Pearson's Canal Companion

PENNINE WATERS

Published by Central Waterways Supplies of Rugby
Tel/fax 01788 546692 email: *sales@centralwaterways.co.uk*
Third edition 2004. ISBN 0 9545383 4 X
Printed in Italy by STIGE of Torino

tiller**man**

By gum it's good to be back 'Up North', where the chip shops are called 'fisheries' and pork pies served warm with liquid jelly. Guidebook compilers are serial adulterers, making eyes at one landscape after another; troubadours of minutiae, harbingers of change. But Pearsons can usually hold their heads high, welcomed back like prodigal sons, however sniping they might have been in previous editions.

Research for the third edition of Pennine Waters coincided synchronistically with work on a guide book to the scenic railways of Yorkshire, Lancashire and Cumbria*. From time to time, wandering the streets of say Saltaire or Gargrave, it was difficult to remember whether you had to get back to the station or the canal. But at least the overlap reinforced the long held belief that such places are amongst the most refreshing, inspiring and downright entertaining in the British Isles, and that - in boating terms at least - their relative lack of popularity is as mystifying as it is perverse.

It was good, however, to see the Huddersfield Canal attracting more boaters. Restoring the Huddersfield Narrow Canal has brought fresh impetus and newly acquired pride to communities in Yorkshire's Colne Valley and Greater Manchester's Tameside, perfectly illustrating how invigorating canals can be, whether you're directly involved or simply value them as somewhere to walk the dog - with a poop-scoop of course!

Michael Pearson

*Iron Roads North of Leeds
ISBN 0 9545383 5 8

6

The
LEEDS & LIVERPOOL
Canal

WHETHER Wigan marks the beginning, or the end, of your exploration of the canals of the Pennines, it is not the kind of place that can be easily erased from your memory. If there is a more gruelling, less edifying flight of locks in the country, it does not spring readily to mind. Not only does each chamber consist of four heavily mitred gates, but each of six sets of paddle gear (two ground, four gate) is hand-cuff locked as a security measure against vandalism. Nevertheless, you may begin to derive a perverse enjoyment from the half day or so that boating up or down the flight will take. Gain from the experience. It's the sort of journey you will probably only make once in a lifetime, though whether you'll ever boast proudly of it as 'my holiday of a lifetime', remains to be seen.

In our CHESHIRE RING Canal Companion we suggest imagining the sound of clogs on cobbles at Wigan Pier, and that seems as good a point as any to begin this Pennine Journey. Leaving astern Wigan's heartland of textile mills, the Leeds & Liverpool Canal's main line passes the junction of its branch to Leigh (and thence the Bridgewater Canal link with Manchester) and commences a climb in excess of two hundred feet in less than two miles up to the level of the old Lancaster Canal. Railway bridges frame the first lock - the eighty-fifth from Leeds, but twenty-first from the top - which sets the tone for the whole flight. Steadily you begin to accumulate locks under your belt. In the momentum of your journey they begin to lose individuality. The slender, slightly warped spire of St Catherine's church proves a stubborn landmark, seemingly in no hurry to come closer or grow distant depending on your direction of travel. St Patrick's amateur rugby league ground and little streets with the whiff of the 19th century about them overlook the canal between locks 80 and 81, whilst in the following pound, neat new industrial units provoke piquant contrast with the sooty walls of an old works beyond. The past cannot be so easily expunged. Bat an eyelid, and a 'Wiganer' might easily glide out of the next chamber loaded to the gunnels with coal. New housing gathers beside locks 77 and 78 and the canal environment has been landscaped with a tiled

From Manchester ("Cheshire Ring")
From Liverpool

Wigan

Girobank

WIGAN

1 The Way We Were
2 The Orwell
3 Terminal Warehouse
4 Wigan Pier
5 Trencherfield Mill Museum of Memories

Pottery Road
Wallgate

BW

Town Centre

Wigan Locks No.s 65-87
214ft 7ins

Wigan Bakery

Crawford Arms

golf course

Haigh Hall Country Park

Red Rock

B5239

B5238 to Aspull

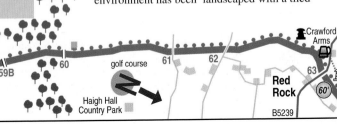

towpath and neatly grassed verge. Such cosmetic improvements provide a metaphor for Wigan itself: lean, gaunt and partially refurbished. A high slag heap looms over Lock 73. The locals call it 'Rabbit Rocks' and it was made from the waste material of Kirkless Iron & Steel Works which occupied the neighbouring wastelands between 1858 and 1931. Scramble to the top for panoramic views over Wigan and northwards to Winter Hill and Rivington Pike. The trackbed of the old Lancashire Union Railway has been converted into a creditable footpath signposted "Haigh Country Park". Bridge 56 is inscribed '1816' and gives access to Kirkless Hall, a partially half-timbered farmhouse predating the industrialism of Wigan.

A pair of canalside pubs make a welcome sight as the flight reaches its logical conclusion. Top Lock is also known as Aspull Lock. It is overlooked by a lock-keeper's cottage, a small office and, to the rear, old stabling. Facilities include water, Elsan, refuse disposal and public toilets. Spend a few minutes exploring. Go and gaze over the parapet of Bridge 59, along what was to have been the line of the Lancaster Canal on its way to join the Bridgewater at Westhoughton near Worsley, before the money ran out.

Journeying eastwards (though north-west at first) urban Wigan is quickly exchanged for a predominantly rural landscape, there being no development beyond the B5238. By bridge 59A there are suggestions of a former wharf and, nearby, a curiously bell-towered stone house. The canal rides along a low escarpment providing views westwards as far as the cooling towers of Fiddlers Ferry power station on the banks of the Mersey. The grounds of Haigh Hall spill down to the waterside. There is a serene passage through woodland, with an elegant footbridge throwing its graceful, lattice span over the cut adjacent to a small, reedy basin replete with stone side bridge, probably provided for goods destined for use at the hall. Haigh Hall itself is now a municipal amenity, more or less masked by trees beyond a golf course which accompanies the canal for some way.

Water lilies thrive in the vicinity of bridge 61. At RED ROCK the main Euston-Glasgow railway is momentarily visible in the valley of the Douglas, and the spire of Standish church punctures the horizon. Pleasant visitor moorings are provided to the north of bridge 63 where there are remains of an old coal tippler. The hillsides beyond the river were once extensively opencast mined and presumably the canal accommodated some of this trade.

Bridge 57, Wigan Locks

9

*L*OCK-free, and crossing the boundary between Greater Manchester and Lancashire, the 'Lancaster Pool' essays a serpentine course, revelling in peaceful countryside, with many stretches richly wooded. Arley Hall, now a golf clubhouse, is surrounded by a moat. Red House Aqueduct carries the canal across the River Douglas. After rain (and by gum did it rain when we came along here) the river water gushes down between its high banks like the Charge of the Light Brigade. The extensive White Bear Marina occupies the site of White Bear railway station, whilst the painted gable end of the old Adlington Industrial Co-op Bakery mournfully overlooks a small, canalside park provided with useful visitor moorings.

ADLINGTON itself introduces some welcome variety to the canal's woodland wanderings. To the east, Pennine moorlands rise up in waves of Lowry-like loneliness and solitude-evoking imagery. The tower on Rivington Pike is backed by Winter Hill and its radio masts. Pike Tower has been an East Lancashire landmark since it was erected in the 18th century. It stands on a summit 1200ft above sea level and on a clear day you can see the Isle of Man from here. For a number of years it belonged to Lord Leverhulme of "Sunlight Soap" fame. A fell-runners' race to the Pike takes place every Easter Saturday.

Another boatyard, squeezed into a narrow cutting alongside the A6 trunk road from London to Carlisle, brings activity to the canal in the vicinity of Heath Charnock. The course of an abandoned railway leads to the site of Duxbury Park and Ellerbeck collieries. The former was closed by its owners during the Depression before being rescued and re-opened by its workforce, thereafter remaining open until 1965. So much coal was carried along the canal that, when the water was drained for maintenance, local people would rush out and pick (or 'kebb' in the local vernacular) any spilt coal from the bed of the canal.

On the A6, adjacent to Bridge 73, stands Frederick's ice cream parlour. A family business of Italian descent, the company has been making ice cream (as only the Italians know how) in Chorley since 1892. Now they boast over seventy flavours made on these Bolton Road premises, though real ice cream enthusiasts will admit that vanilla has never been bettered. Even today, Frederick's 'top secret' ingredients are imported from Italy.

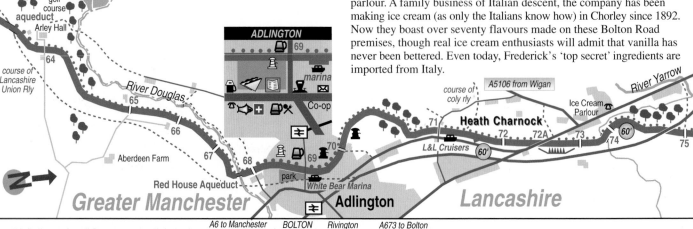

THE canal treats Chorley rather disdainfully, skirting the eastern rim of the town, so that all the inland navigator gets to see is a periphery of mills and housing estates. At Botany Bay a large mill has been converted into a slightly surreal antiques centre. Equally unusual, a landmark on the neighbouring hillside is the Preston Temple of the Church of Latter Day Saints.

JOHNSON'S HILLOCK LOCKS may be a bit tongue-twisting, but they combine to create a gorgeous flight of seven chambers, carrying the 'real' Leeds & Liverpool Canal down to (or up from) the Lancaster Canal's original route. Setting off in the direction of its old summit at Walton, the Lancaster peters out in the vicinity of Whittle-le-Woods, a good deal of its course having been submerged beneath the M61. At Walton cargoes were transhipped from barge on to tramway wagons and taken across the steeply-sided Ribble Valley before being arduously floated once again at Preston Basin.

But back to the delights of Johnson's Hillock, where the immaculately coiffured chambers are separated, each from the other - towards the foot of the flight at least - by broad glassy pools. A grassy path winds through buttercup and clover meadows grazed by congenial geldings on the offside, crossing by-weirs on neat little timber footbridges which contribute much to the beauty of the scene.

Above the locks, the canal curves around the steep-sided valley of the River Lostock. Banks of gorse line the cut. Herons patrol their beats along the canal bank. Rolling sheep pastures and ribbons of woodland combine to create a soothing landscape for the canal to lose itself in. Peace reigns supreme in what amounts to a surprising vacuum of agricultural land between the old textile centres of East Lancs.

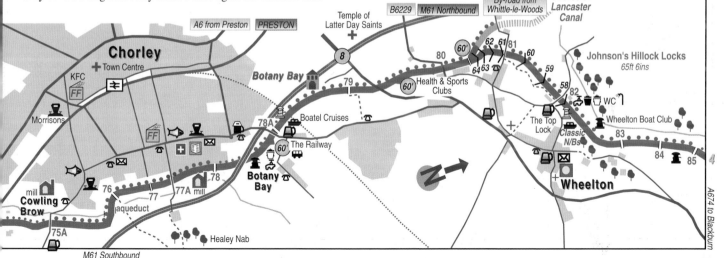

11

Evening stroll, Johnson's Hillock Locks

CROSSING the watershed between the rivers Lostock and Darwen - both tributaries of the Ribble, though not destined to meet before the estuary - the canal traverses a largely rural landscape whose only brush with urbanisation is the suburbs of Feniscowles. By Bridge 87 a steep sided clough all but hides an enigmatic, high-vaulted bridge which might almost be carrying a second canal. No other guide, past or present, we could lay our hands on, even mentions it. Trust Pearsons to have the facts at their fingertips! It's the Thirlmere water supply aqueduct, opened in 1894 to bring water a hundred miles from the Lake District to Manchester.

As publishers, papermaking is a subject close to our hearts, though it is hardly any longer a significant facet of British Industry. Many mills have closed. Those that haven't tend to be in foreign ownership. East Lancs was a notable centre of papermaking and the Leeds & Liverpool played an important role in transporting raw materials and fuel to the works and the finished product away. These days the canal reflects metaphorically - and sometimes quite literally - the fickle fortunes of the paper industry. At WITHNELL FOLD a mill which once produced bank-note paper for currencies throughout the civilized world has been colonised

by sundry light industries. Forty-eight hour visitor moorings exist in the shadow of the mill and you could well fill those hours exploring the vicinity of this charming backwater. Beyond the towpath wall the land falls suddenly away to a series of filter beds which have been transformed into a nature reserve, a primeval paradise of dragonflies, water lilies and dipping pools. In the opposite direction a stroll up the cobbled lane from bridge 88 introduces you to a 'model' village of paper-workers' cottages and a piquant little green with a sundial as its centrepiece; a moving memorial to the local men who didn't march home from two world wars.

Despite the concerted protests of 'tree people', the M65 was built across the canal in 1995. At Bridge 91A the Boatyard Inn (Tel: 01254 209841) is a modern pub occupying the site of an old short-boat building yard. The paper industry rears its high-chimnied head again between bridges 92 and 93B. Coal came in by barge and you can still see the mooring rings and evidence of an aerial ropeway employed to carry the coal from the canal bank into the works.

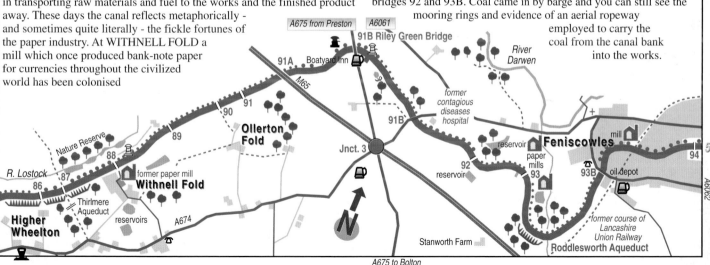

BLACKBURN impinges its urban - though not necessarily urbane - personality on the canal, obliterating all sense of countryside for the best part of five miles. There are still, however, green horizons to savour: Jubilee Tower on Darwen Hill to the south; the woodlands of Witton Country Park to the north. But this is primarily a part of the journey which should be devoted to disinterring the remains of King Cotton; though it must be emphasised that the local authority have not been content to live in the past, and a good deal of work has been undertaken to revitalise Blackburn's canal corridor: if only the hooligans would refrain from vandalising the improvements the moment that they are made.

Every Sixties adolescent remembers from *Sgt. Pepper* that there were

"Four thousand holes in Blackburn, Lancashire." But once there were two hundred factory chimneys as well, one of them, at 312ft, probably the highest in the UK, stood canalside at Bennington Street refuse works, built in 1888 of nearby Accrington's famously durable bricks. Durable, but dynamitable, and now you can count Blackburn's post industrial smoke stacks on your fingers. Many mills have shuffled off their mortal coil, or found new uses - a pub in the Albion, television news studios at Daisyfield - but pride of place remains with the massive Imperial Mill by bridge 104A, a vast, sprawling, redbrick, zinc-domed dinosaur hanging on for dear life. In 1910 there were 87,377 looms in the town operated by 42,000 dexterous textile workers, many of them children as young as twelve.

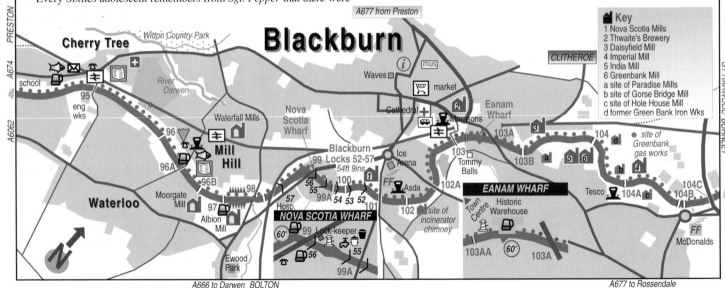

Key
1 Nova Scotia Mills
2 Thwaite's Brewery
3 Daisyfield Mill
4 Imperial Mill
5 India Mill
6 Greenbank Mill
a site of Paradise Mills
b site of Gorse Bridge Mill
c site of Hole House Mill
d former Green Bank Iron Wks

Crossing an embankment on the western edge of town, Ewood Park football stadium soars above humble terraced rooftops. In common with many Lancashire clubs, Blackburn Rovers' history goes back to the dawn of professional football. They were First Division champions twice in the years leading up to the First World War, and FA Cup winners on six occasions. After a period in the footballing wilderness, they came to prominence again in 1995, winning the Premiership under the management of Kenny Dalglish with a team which included Alan Shearer and David Batty, built from millions invested by the local steel magnate Jack Walker. Sadly, Blackburn's footballing sugar daddy has gone to that great stadium in the sky since the heady days of the championship, but Blackburn, under the astute management of former Liverpool star, Graeme Souness, remain well-established as a Premiership side.

A flight of six locks carries the canal up on to its elevated position on the western edge of town. A lock-keeper resides at NOVA SCOTIA WHARF where the Groundwork Trust have refurbished former stables and workshops, and where the provision of water and refuse disposal provides boaters with theoretically secure moorings for a stopover in Blackburn; though when we were here the Groundwork Trust offices had most of their windows boarded up as if they'd just been the victims of a rather nasty attack of window smashing. As we have observed before, local authorities should do more to provide boaters with reassuring facilities for overnight stays. In Blackburn's case, they represent the majority of tourist, as opposed to business, visitors to the town, and much more should be done to make them welcome. Researching the first edition, we were 'welcomed' at Eanam Wharf by a gentleman objecting to our mooring in front of his house. Wishing to avoid a local incident, we reversed beneath the warehouse canopy, tied-up alongside the wide boat *Kennet*, and sought advice from the council office within. "Yes, you're OK to moor here, but you'll be locked in after four-thirty, unless you've got a BW handcuff key". We had; so, so far, so good. Then we discovered that it was only feasible to unlock the gate from the outside. Fortunately, we numbered amongst our crew, an exile from the Polish State Circus, agile enough to circumnavigate the wrought-iron 'security' fence and let us out. But what a palaver. Little wonder boaters think twice about stopping at Blackburn. In the event we spent a peaceful night, undisturbed until the arrival, at eight-thirty next morning, of the crew of a maintenance boat moored alongside (for similar considerations of security) the evening before.

Overlooked by a plethora of mills, and providing a fascinating panoramic view of the town - notably its cathedral and Thwaite's brewery, those twin religions of god and beer - the canal zig-zags around the eastern fringe of the centre. Audley Bridge (102A) appears to have been reinforced with girders cast as far afield as Darlington in 1878; perhaps with Blackburn's soon to be developed tramway system in mind. The trams are long gone, and the once massive railway station has been rebuilt more modestly too, a 'bubble-wrap' canopy replacing its formerly barn like roofs. Do cock an ear for a distant whistle, however, for this is often the route of steam excursions heading to and from the famous Settle & Carlisle line.

Extensive coal wharves once abutted both sides of Cicely Street Bridge (103) and a travelling crane facilitated fast turnrounds for discharging barges. Tommy Ball's shoe emporium occupies the site of Alma cotton mill, access from the towpath being by way of a footbridge spanning the canal at EANAM WHARF, one of the Leeds & Liverpool's most significant goods depots. Twenty-five thousand natives gathered to see its opening in 1810. The local rag's 'shipping list' for the 27th June of that year quotes the arrival of the barges *Dispatch* carrying yarn, molasses and tallow; *Defiance* with timber and lead; and *Ten Sisters* bearing malt and earthenware. A hundred and forty-five years later John Seymour arrived here aboard his converted Dutch sailing barge *Jenny the Third* (*Sailing Through England*, Eyre & Spottiswoode 1956) and found the depot stuffed with cotton bales brought by lorry from Liverpool docks. For short boats, wide boats - call them what you will - the writing was already on the wall.

Between bridges 103A and 104A the emphasis is overtly industrial. Paradise Bridge (103B) seems somewhat ironically named unless you are deeply into industrial archaeology. Evidence of the emasculation of heavy industry is evinced by bridge 104A where the Furthergate Chemical Works has become a Tesco superstore: the young turks of East Lancashire stacking shelves with artichokes and anchovies where their grandfathers superintended the production of chlorines and hydrocarbonates.

BLACKBURN

60' 106

site of brick works

60'

site of quarry wharf

107

Cut Farm

site of Fire Clay works

107A

course of Lancs & Yorks Rly Gt Harwood Loop

playing fields

108

sites of former textile mills

site of Whitebirk power station

5
(105)

A678

Rishton Reservoir

Rishton

108A

M65

Bridge 112, Church

Oakenshaw

114B

60'

golf course

60'

aqueduct

Dunkenhalgh Hotel

Enfield Wharf

Clayton Le Moors

114C

114A

114AA

Moorfield Coly & Coke wks

115

115A
(pipe)

M65

109

7

114

site of Aspen Coly. & Coke wks.

site of quarry wharf

113

60'

site of old coly

cricket ground

Enfield

113A

school

school

cemetery

course of former mineral rlys

112

110

William Blythe chem wks

111

Church
Church Wharf

Peel Arm

Dill Hall

schools

N

WEST End

111D

Milnshaw

Church Wharf

B6231 to Oswaldtwistle

Accrington Town Centre   A680 to Accrington

CONTRIVING to double the crow-flying distance between Blackburn and Clayton, the Leeds & Liverpool curves voluptuously with the contours, the canal equivalent of a Renoir nude. In cargo-carrying days this profligacy with the miles may have irked, but now we are grateful for as much of this invigorating and stimulating canal journey as we can get; valuing its long-windedness, letting the Calder Valley motorway cater for the speed merchants.

Blackburn becomes a memory. A bland retail park replaces Whitebirk Power Station, source of the last regular trade on this section of the canal, until the thirteen-week freeze of '63 finally convinced the Electricity Generating Board of the inefficacy of canal transport. The power station had been built in 1921 on the site of a plantation. Coal was discharged from barges on the offside - a wasteground of saplings now - and conveyed overhead into the plant on the towpath side of the canal. The bulk of Whitebirk's coal came from Bank Hall Colliery at Burnley (a lockless 15 miles to the east), but a proportion also originated from pits in the Wigan coalfield. They stopped making the sparks fly here in 1976 and the power station was demolished seven years later.

Around the next bend quarrying brought traffic to the canal, tramways linking the cut with workfaces on the hillside. Evidence of such wharves remains along with ramps cut into the canal bank to simplify the recovery of boat horses which had fallen into the water. Rishton Reservoir was built in 1828 to augment water supplies to the western end of the canal. The Blackburn - Burnley railway crosses its southern end by causeway. The old loop line to Great Harwood closed to passenger trains in 1957. Canon Roger Lloyd, one of many clergymen with a deep interest in railways, wrote of it in *Farewell to Steam*, recalling that when he was vicar at Great Harwood in the Twenties, 75% of the working population were unemployed and on the Means Test.

Exhilaratingly androgynous, the landscape combines the feminine allure of pastures backed by waves of moorland, with the masculinity of industry and urbanisation. Chameleon-like, the canal seems to alter its character and sexual persuasion in response to its environment. RISHTON is imbued with XY chromosomes, and though its gaunt mills have tumbled, tightly-packed terraced streets remain.

A concrete aqueduct carries the canal over the motorway. Down there on that tarmac they are travelling so rapidly that they can avoid the need to think altogether. Shunning this example, the canal traveller circumnavigates the community of CHURCH: though take to the path which swoops down into the Aspen valley between bridges 109 and 112 and you can beat the boat with ease. Now carried on an embankment, when the East Lancs Railway was built in 1848, the line crossed the valley on a lengthy timber viaduct. It took twenty years of spoil-tipping to bury the bridge. Aspen Colliery opened in 1869. Coke was produced in a series of 'beehive' ovens, traces of which remain beside a reed-filled basin adjacent to the railway. Once there were fifteen mines in the neighbourhood of Church and Oswaldtwistle. Chemical production is another local industry. William Blythe's are still flourishing a hundred and fifty years after the said Mr Blythe, a canny Scot from Kirkcaldy, set up in business, attracted by the canal's transport potential.

A substantial, three-storey canal warehouse overlooks a right-angle bend in the canal at Church Wharf. Flyboats once unloaded cotton here, and despite the ruined state of the building, still seem almost tangible. St James's church marks the halfway point between Liverpool and Leeds. Eastbound boaters encounter their first swing-bridges: familiarity will breed not so much contempt as a deep and lasting loathing. There were proposals, towards the end of the 19th century, to extend the Peel Arm (dug initially to serve a calico works) into the centre of Accrington, but sadly (for Accrington is a fascinating place) they never came to fruition.

ENFIELD WHARF marked a hiatus in the canal's westbound construction for several years while more capital was raised. No longer does it play host to Hydburn Sea Scouts and its warehouses wait - probably hopelessly - for a new use. We looked in vain for Appleby's flour mill, operators, once, of a fleet of barges, and the soap factory which specialised in the production of 'floating soap'. Briefly rubbing shoulders with suburbia, the Leeds & Liverpool is soon out into open country east of Clayton, a community not quite so bucolic as its name implies. The comedian, Eric Morecambe, worked as a Bevan Boy at Moorfield Colliery during the Second World War. Not so amusingly, the mine was the scene of an undergound explosion in 1883, causing the deaths of sixty-eight workers including boys as young as ten. Now its site, and that of the adjoining coke works, is being developed as an industrial estate.

YES, those are *green* fields lapping at the margins of the cut, stretching from the towpath's drystone wall boundary to a horizon of moorlands, the Calder Valley, Trough of Bowland and Pendle Hill. Savour them, for there is an inevitability about the onslaught of Burnley and Blackburn.

Southwards, the quarry-scalloped edge of Great Hameldon (1343ft) prefaces the lonely tops of the Forest of Rossendale. But the motorway effectively curtails the proximity of this landscape, and it is northwards, over the valley of the Calder (no relation to the navigable West Riding namesake, though born of the same watershed) that the canal traveller's eye tends to be drawn. You may even catch glimpses of Penyghent in the wide blue yonder. In the middle distance the parkland demesnes of Read, Simonstone and Huntroyde contrast with stone-walled pastures patterned by darker masses of woodland, ascending to the mottled flanks of Pendleton Moor. Nearer at hand the canal arcs to cross a series of ravines, or cloughs as they call them hereabouts, gouged out by watercourses cascading down to the Calder. The road from Bridge 118 leads to a rather good Jennings pub in Altham called The Walton Arms - Tel: 01282 774444.

In Altham Clough Wood old maps locate the existence of coal pits. And indeed, for such a comparatively rural setting, there is much for the diligent industrial archaeologist to uncover. The site, for example of Altham Vitriol Works; the enigmatic canalside ruin at Lower Clough Bank; the remains of Altham Brick & Tile Works; Castle Clough Dyeworks and the vanished Perseverance Mill at Hapton must all have stories to tell if only we had the space and the time.

Between Hapton and Rose Grove the canal was diverted to facilitate construction of the motorway. This end of the old Great Harwood Loop Line railway has only recently been lifted following the cessation of coal carrying to Padiham's now demolished power station. Rose Grove has railway resonances too, for here, on a site now largely buried beneath the M65, was one of the last three motive power depots retained to service steam until August 1968. The locomotives took their water from the canal, and it was said that they could always tell a Rose Grove tender when it went to the works by the shoals of minnows inside. British Waterways have a maintenance base in a restored warehouse by bridge 126A. This is a good, secure place to moor overnight with showers and the usual facilities on site.

IKE an immigration officer slamming a hairy fist down on your passport, Burnley embosses a distinct impression on the Leeds & Liverpool Canal as it curves coruscatingly from one fresh view to another, seemingly determined to disembowel Burnley and pick over its entrails. And entrails don't come much juicier to predatory industrial archaeologists than the textile town's famous Weaver's Triangle, a dense conglomerate of mills and weaving sheds gathered on the banks of the waterway which kick-started its 19th century zenith of prosperity. Between bridges 129B and 130B the canal is at its most scintillating as it weaves -

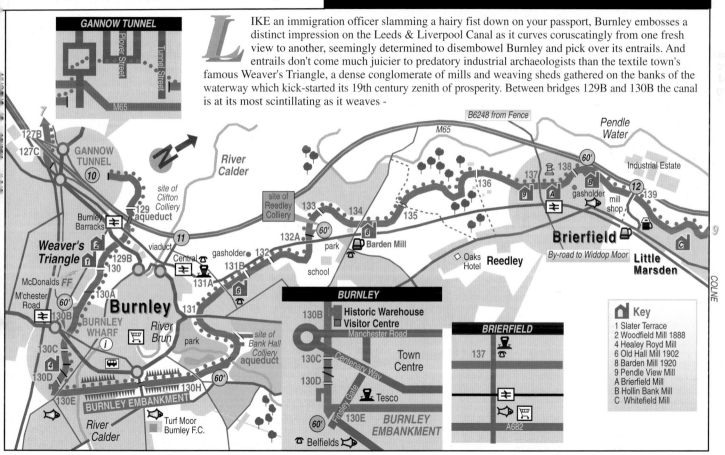

Key
1 Slater Terrace
2 Woodfield Mill 1888
4 Healey Royd Mill
6 Old Hall Mill 1902
8 Barden Mill 1920
9 Pendle View Mill
A Brierfield Mill
B Hollin Bank Mill
C Whitefield Mill

forgive the pun - between man-made canyons of lofty mills. Of unique interest, are the premises by bridge 130, where a ground floor workshop is topped by a terrace of two-storey workers' cottages accessed by a balcony incorporating a cast-iron balustrade. Wake at dawn, and all you had to do was go downstairs to work. Cunning devils, the bosses, disguising this arrangement as altruism.

The canal's western entry into Burnley is by way of GANNOW TUNNEL, a towpathless, 559 yards long bore which forces towpath walkers to traverse a potentially bewildering network of motorway underpasses and terraced streets. Lucky you have your Canal Companion with you and the enlargement on Map 8 which reveals all.

Manchester Road climbs up from Burnley's Town Hall and celebrated Mechanics Institute to BURNLEY WHARF with its imposing warehouses and overhanging canopy betraying a family resemblance to Eanam Wharf at Blackburn. If anything, this Burnley example is even more impressive and makes a fitting location for the Weaver's Triangle visitor centre housed in the wharf-master's house and toll office. FINSLEY GATE WHARF continues to blight the scene, no entrepreneurs seemingly tempted yet by its 'exciting development potential'.

Mills, wharves, tunnels: all good clean fun, but Burnley's most astonishing canal gesture, and one of Robert Aickman's *Seven Wonders of the Waterways*, is the embankment which carries the Leeds & Liverpool across the broad, converging valleys of the Calder and Brun, to the east of the town centre. Sixty feet high, and three-quarters of a mile long, BURNLEY EMBANKMENT affords the canal traveller a bird's eye view of the town: a seemingly endless railway viaduct; the bus park; Turf Moor football stadium where Burnley, a club with a pedigree as proud as Blackburn's down the cut, were languishing in the First Division when we last passed through; slate rooftops of densely packed terraced streets which gleam dully after a shower like tarnished silver; a largely petrified forest of factory chimneys; and all this horizoned by backdrops of wild moorland; an escape clause for all those consigned to an occluded existence in these Pennine textile towns. On one of the tops to the south-east a wind farm gesticulates madly.

North of the embankment the canal skirts a pretty municipal park and crosses an aqueduct carrying it over the River Brun, one of the shortest rivers we can think of, rising on the flanks of Worsthorne Moor, just three or four miles to the east, and colliding with the Calder in some obscure corner of Burnley town centre. The "Burnley Way", a forty mile footpath circling the district, follows the Brun upstream from here. In earlier times a mineral railway serving Bank Hall Colliery passed beneath the aqueduct. The mine's barge loading basin is still in water by the sharp turn in the canal, as is a former drydock nearby. Bank Hall's first shaft was sunk in 1860, but perhaps its busiest period for canal traffic was in the middle of the twentieth century when it was the principal supplier of coal to Whitebirk power station at Blackburn. The pit was finally closed in 1972 on safety grounds.

The canal makes its northern exit from Burnley past dwindling numbers of textile mills. The single-track railway to Colne comes alongside. By the railway bridge (132A) the canal widens at the site of Reedley Colliery loading basin. At Bridge 134 Barden Mill is enjoying a new lease of life as a retail centre which provides moorings (and even water if you ask them nicely at the checkout) and a comfortable restaurant. Between here and Brierfield the waterway surfaces for a gulp of fresh air. Good honest countryside intervenes, and a quality of remoteness, heightened by the proximity of urbanisation. Pendle Hill (1831ft) looks good from this angle, and the villages cuddled in the folds of its south-facing flank hold memories of the notorious Lancashire Witches. But at BRIERFIELD the mills comeback, two of the largest engaged in the lucrative business of producing medical gauze.

Weaver's Triangle, Burnley

CATHARSIS comes to the cut. Depending on your direction of travel, you are about to exchange the satanic textile towns of East Lancashire with the wide open spaces of rural Pendle, or vice versa. NELSON churns down its hillside to the canal bank in a vortex of mills and still-cobbled streets. Your subconscious is disappointed not to come upon George Formby "leaning on a lamppost at the corner of a street", even if these days any "certain little lady" going by is likely to be of Asian descent; though her dialect will remain disarmingly Pennine.

It must be disorientating to live in 19th century streets like these with out of town retail parks just a magic carpet ride down the motorway. But our old friends the industrial archaeologists will be having a field day picking over the finer points of mill chimney decoration and lost in admiration for the restored three-storey

warehouse at Yarnspinner's Wharf by bridge 141A, a brick-built cousin of the structures at Burnley and Blackburn which has at last found a new use for itself as part of a health centre. Bridge 141B is overlooked by Seed Mills where carpet yarn is spun, and, on the towpath side, the engine house of the Pendle Street Power Co dated 1885.

Pendle Hill continues to provide the thematic sub-text to your journey, poking its nose in whenever there's a lapse in industry's small talk. BARROWFORD LOCKS, popular with sightseers, carry the canal some seventy feet up out of the valley of the Colne and Pendle waters to its six mile summit pound, four hundred and eighty-seven feet above sea level. The flight derives its name from the weaving village to the west, whilst the important town of Colne straddles a hillside in the

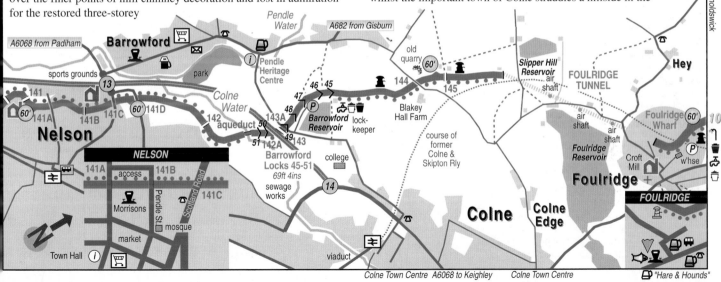

Greenberfield Top Lock

opposite direction, the clocktower of its town hall dominating the view against the moorland backdrop of the Forest of Trawden. Less than ten miles over there lies Haworth and Bronteland.

Back alongside the canal, Barrowford Reservoir receives what excess water the summit might have to offer. A small car park is provided for motorised visitors to the flight. Blacko Tower overlooks proceedings. It was erected in 1890 by a grocer called Jonathan Stansfield who preferred follies to women and alcohol. He may have had a point.

Pleasant farmland intervenes between Barrowford top lock and the western portal of Foulridge's celebrated tunnel. The 1,640 yards long tunnel's claim to fame lies not so much in the fact that it is the longest on the Leeds & Liverpool Canal, but that it was the scene, in 1912, of one of the more bizarre events in the annals of bovine history, when a cow called Buttercup fell into the canal at the western end of the tunnel and swam through to the eastern end before being rescued and revived with brandy.

Towpathless, and confined to one-way working, FOULRIDGE TUNNEL was five long years in the making, the cut & cover technique being applied. Leggers gave way to steam tugs in 1880, which in turn survived until 1937, by which time trade over the top was negligible and largely diesel-powered in any case. Colour-light signals control the entry of boats through the tunnel, turning green for ten minutes on the half-hour at the western end and likewise on the hour at the eastern end. Thirty minutes are allowed for passage through the tunnel. Walkers must make their way over the top, the trackbed of the old Colne & Skipton railway providing a useful footpath, though sticky in places, and after prolonged periods of wet weather the local lanes are probably preferable.

FOULRIDGE WHARF is a magnet for the boater and the land-based canal enthusiast alike. A trip boat plys from here and British Waterways were in the process of erecting a new boating facilities block as we went to press. A well-preserved stone warehouse (with Leeds & Liverpool Carrying Co still perceptible on its gable end) adds dignity to the scene, but the unusual trestle railway bridge carrying the course of the Colne & Skipton railway has sadly been demolished. In many respects the highlight of the wharf is a restored limekiln erected early in the construction of the canal to provide lime for mortar, which relied initially on Lothersdale limestone brought in by 'lime gals'. Not, to some of our crew's regret, stocky local wenches with descendents in the vicinity, but sturdy Galloway ponies.

THERE really should be some ceremonial equivalent on the Leeds & Liverpool of the crossing of the equator as one passes from Lancashire to Yorkshire; from the land of Gracie Fields to the land of Geoffrey Boycott. Meddlesome politicians arranged for the time honoured boundary to be moved in 1974. Prior to that it crossed the canal between bridges 149 and 150 where a feeder from Whitemoor Reservoir enters the canal overlooked by a big stone mill with attractive employees houses alongside. Barnoldswick apart, with its Rolls Royce plants (where Frank Whittle's dreams of jet propulsion really *took off*), the Ouzledale foundry which makes Esse cookers, and the Silent Night bed factory housed partially in an old canalside textile mill, the canal's journey is predominantly rustic in character.

Scar tissue from abandoned canal and railway branches can still be discerned. The Rain Hall Rock canal was cut to expedite the extraction of limestone from an aquatic, linear quarry face. In its half mile it included two short tunnels and a viaduct carrying a by-road. Unfortunately, most of its remains have been buried by landfill. 'Barlick' lost its shuttle train service from nearby Earby in 1965. Apparently it was nicknamed 'The Spud'. You can buy an attractive set of postcards of it in its death throes at the TIC.

A chunk of the bridge which carried it over the canal remains like a half-eaten apple. The canal shop at Lower Park Marina has the reputation of being the best of its kind in the north.

GREENBERFIELD LOCKS are exquisite and compulsively photogenic. Three single chambers replaced a time-consuming staircase early in the nineteenth century, remains of which can still be seen, including a bridge-hole niftily commandeered as a stable. By the top lock a feeder comes in from Winterburn Reservoir. A picnic site (with refreshment kiosk) is provided for motorists and use of the towpath is boosted by walkers on the "Pendle Way". Greenberfield was to have been the departure point for a branch canal proposed to link the main line with the market town of Settle. The mind boggles with the beauty of what might have been. A dwelling in Settle bears the name "Liverpool House" in anticipation of the canal which never came. To the north the horizon extends to infinity in waves of moorland.

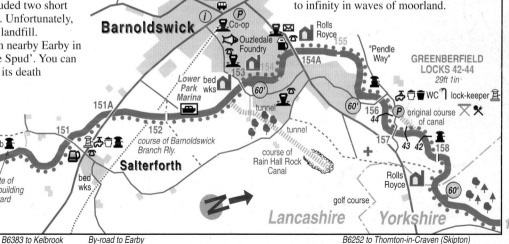

feeder from Whitemoor Res.

Bancroft Mill

Barnoldswick

Co-op

Ouzledale Foundry

Rolls Royce

"Pendle Way"

GREENBERFIELD LOCKS 42-44
29ft 1in

WC   lock-keeper

Lower Park Marina

bed wks

149   mill

150

Boat Club

site of boatbuilding yard

147   148

sewage plant

151   151A

152

bed wks

Salterforth

course of Barnoldswick Branch Rly.

153   154   154A

155

156   original course of canal

157

43   42   158

44

tunnel

tunnel

course of Rain Hall Rock Canal

golf course

Rolls Royce

Lancashire   **Yorkshire**

*T*HEY say that the only man-made object which astronauts can make out on the earth's surface is the Great Wall of China. But it is difficult to believe that they cannot also see this dizzy, disorientating, peregrinating pool of Marton wriggling and writhing across the upland pastures of the Yorkshire Dales. We enjoyed an idyllic day of boating, fine-judging its bindweed bends, a March sun warm on our backs, lapwings and curlews calling overhead.

This is drumlin country. The propensity of the Ice Age's retreating glaciers to leave their litter behind them has left us with a legacy of profound beauty, for these smooth rounded hillocks are as ravishing as the fleshy contours of the woman in your life. In many respects, Marton Pool is bound to remind seasoned canal travellers of the Oxford Canal's summit; it even has a transmitter mast which seems determined to baffle your sense of direction, and similarly there are moments of confusion when you glimpse what appears to be a boat on another parallel-running canal, only to discover that it is the same canal re-inventing itself time after time.

One could easily be beguiled into mooring up at EAST MARTON forever. All life's essentials are here. A country pub; a cosy cafe serving mouth-watering wedges of coffee-cake; and a traditional red telephone kiosk from which you can call your boss and tell him you've quit. Tempted? But the A59's relentless traffic brings with it a sense of reality and responsibilty, even if the double-arched bridge which carries it is one of the little wonders of the waterways, an engagingly beautiful mother of invention whereby the realigned, upgraded road was simply provided with a second arch above the first. Other travellers enjoy a brief encounter with the canal as the Pennine Way appropriates the towpath for half a mile or so of its 256 mile course from Edale to Kirk Yetholm. Exchange a wave with the back-packers. Your goals may differ but your pace is the same. The journey's the thing in both instances, the intoxication of travel for travel's sake.

BANK NEWTON LOCKS lower the canal helter-skelter down into the valley of the Aire above a sprinkling of typical Dales farmsteads from which the pong of slurry is born bucolically upon the breeze. The locks are notable in retaining clough-type ground paddles by their top gates, a refreshing survival flying in the face of uniformity, and so easy to operate compared with the laborious windings of windlass-operated paddle gear.

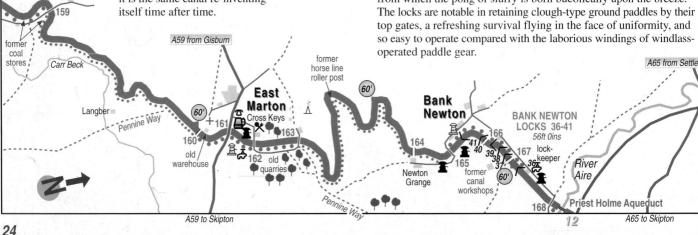

Double-arched bridge, East Marton

Closing the 'clough', Lock 31, Gargrave

MAKING its unfettered way through the deliciously green upper valley of the Aire, the Leeds & Liverpool Canal is overlooked by the russet-coloured crag of Sharp Haw and obelisk-topped Cracoe Fell. GARGRAVE is the only settlement of any significance in what is a surprisingly remote tract of land, especially given the busyness of the A65; West Yorkshire's link with The Lakes. Six locks - almost too dispersed to be considered as a flight - carry the canal through Gargrave, demanding a level of exertion from the boater which can easily be rewarded by a sojourn in this appealing village, for which 3 day visitor moorings are provided above Higher Land Lock.

By bridge 171 an old stone-built warehouse overlooks the canal. One can imagine that it was once stuffed with agricultural produce due to be carried out of the district by barge and coal brought in from the coalfields of East Lancs and West Yorks. Coal is still stocked canalside, in an echo of old trading patterns, but naturally it gets here by lorry now, and no longer from Lancashire or Yorkshire we'll be bound.

On the southern outskirts of Gargrave, Johnson & Johnson's large 'wound management' factory manufactures medical and family hygiene products. We were told that its location in Gargrave is due to the "clean air." With an 'e' or without?

The old Midland Railway's main line to Scotland shares the Aire's broad valley with the road and the canal. Steam specials sometimes use this route on their way to or from the Settle & Carlisle line.

By-road from Grassington

Demesne of Eshton Hall

Eshton Beck

aqueduct

172 172A 60' 60'

Holme Bridge 173

cricket ground

warehouse coal wharf 31 171

Johnson & Johnson

River Aire

170 32

WC 60'

Gargrave House

Pennine Way

169A

Anchor Inn

garden centre

33

34

169 35

viaduct

Gargrave

site of Roman Villa

Thorlby

174

175

A65 from Harrogate

Travel Lodge

school

Skipton Town Centre

Aireville Park

13

A629

A6069

SKIPTON

By-road to Carleton

Inghey Bridge

Earby Beck

course of Skipton & Colne Rly

Locks
30 Holme Bridge Lock 11ft 4ins
31 Low Warehouse Lock 10ft 4ins
32 Higher Land Lock 8ft 0ins
33 Anchor Lock 9ft 2ins
34 Scarland Lock 8ft 7ins
35 Steg Neck lock 10ft 7ins

Pennine Way

N

11 By-road to Broughton A56 to Colne

OVERLOOKED by handsome, avuncular mills - one now engaged in churning out greetings cards, one converted into dignified flats - the canal saunters through Skipton in an amiable frame of mind, throwing off an arm which slips mysteriously beneath the ramparts of the castle to a spooky terminus where barges used to load stone. No craft longer than 35ft can turn at the far end, so those with lengthier vessels unable to resist the temptation to explore this backwater, have to return with their tiller between their legs, in undignified reverse. This SPRINGS BRANCH, can also be followed on foot, providing an inspired short cut to Stanforth's Celebrated Pie Establishment, all but straddling the second bridge up..

A heritage trail of brass rubbing plaques has been erected by British Waterways to elucidate the town's rich canalside past and the towpath facilitates useful short cuts which encourage citizens and visitors alike to embrace the canal instead of turning their back on it. Visitor moorings are available either side of Bridge 178; those to the south border the bus station at a point where wide boats once unloaded gasworks' coal. Bus enthusiasts will relish mooring here if only to enjoy the frequent comings and goings of the grey and orange coloured Leyland National single-deckers operated by Pennine Motors.

South of Skipton the canal winds prettily through Airedale's lush scenery. Bordered by ings - Yorkshire-speak for ground susceptible to flooding - the Aire meanders along its wide valley which rises to ridges topped by moorland scattered with old quarry workings to the east and lead mines to the west, where one or two smelting chimneys remain to remind us of their worked-out trade. Lockless, constant to the 345ft contour, and interspersed with hand-cuff locked swing bridges - of which BRADLEY BRIDGE (182A) is a particularly obstinate example - the waterway parallels the old Keighley and Kendal turnpike which still retains cast iron mileposts considerably more ornate than the Leeds & Liverpool's. Briefly, the canal veers away from the main road to pay court to an old mill village called Low Bradley, then returns to the road and plunges into Farnhill Wood, a good, old-fashioned sort of arboreal glade made up of beech, birch, alder and sycamore growing sturdily out of a floor of moss and fern.

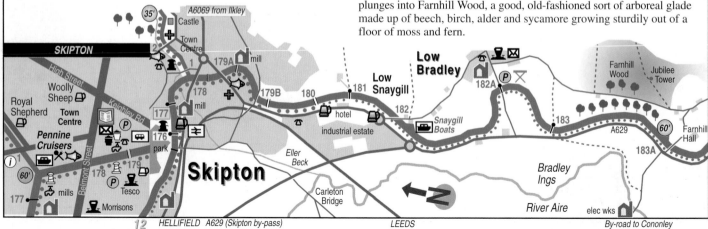

CROSSING the boundary between North and West Yorkshire, the Leeds & Liverpool continues its business partnership with Airedale, evoking visions of curly-haired terriers groomed to perfection to show their paces at Crufts. Every pristine dog has its day. Likewise this gorgeous canal, which conjures up one intoxicating view after another. SILSDEN is a handy point for re-stocking the galley from friendly little throw-back shops where you're still expected to reveal your life history over this grocery transaction or that. In the old days Silsden's Co-op's barge, *Progress*, worked hard on the canal fetching and carrying produce vital to the little mill town's economy. Nowadays the main street reverberates to juggernauts and the canal wharf has become the point of departure for boating holidaymakers; call that 'progress' if you like. At the extremities of this map the canal keeps trysts with fauns and nymphs in glades of ancient woodland. Bandying ancient elixirs, they entice you to stay. Certainly there is no excuse for not scrambling up through the bracken and heather to pay homage to the old Queen's Jubilee Tower on Farnhill Moor. Given balmy weather, the view from the top of the Aire Valley, and its lines of communication is invigorating.

Farnhill and Kildwick are cheek by jowl villages separated only by the slender width of the canal. In fact, Kildwick's churchyard has spilt over on to the Farnhill bank, being linked, appropriately enough, by Parson's Bridge. Here, on a mistbound November day, our research party passed beneath the bridge as a funeral cortege carried a coffin overhead towards a black-caped priest and a throng of mourners waiting beside a freshly-dug grave. We were journeying along the longest canal, but it occurred to us that the occupant of that coffin was making - or had perhaps already made - the longest journey of all.

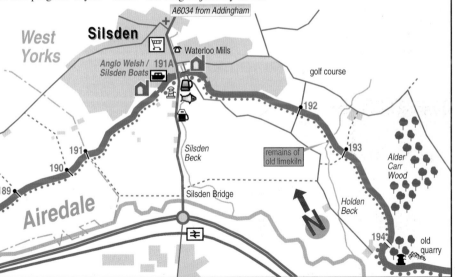

A6034 from Addingham

Silsden

West Yorks

Waterloo Mills

Anglo Welsh / 191A
Silsden Boats

golf course

North Yorks

Farnhill Moor

Jubilee Tower

Crag Top

Farnhill

191

190

189

Silsden Beck

Silsden Bridge

remains of old limekiln

192

193

Alder Carr Wood

Holden Beck

184

185

186 187 60' 188

Kildwick

Airedale

194

old quarry

Farnhill Ings

15

HAPPY-GO-LUCKILY lockless, the canal slots snugly into a ledge above the Aire's suddenly constricted valley, blind to all the blandishments that the kerb-crawling town of Keighley can offer to become better acquainted.

Bridges 197, 197A, 198A and 199 are sophisticated, electrically operated swing affairs, for which you will need a BW sanitary key and some experience in the day to day management of a small power station to open. We were unable to extract the key from one of them and had to abandon it, passing down the canal to rumours of half-mile traffic tail-backs and a motorist's whip-round to pay for a contract to be put out on the boat crew responsible. British Waterways were more magnanimous, admitting that the electrified bridges were prone to malfunction, especially early in the season, before they had got, so to speak, into the 'swing' of things.

At Stockbridge substantial warehouses - which have recently been refurbished for domestic use - recall an era when canal transport played an effective role in Keighley's economy. Wool and sugar were still being carried over the summit from Liverpool docks to these extensive premises in the early Fifties, an activity rudely interrupted on 17th May 1952 by a massive breach in the canal's bank which all but washed away the local golf course. Luckily, three maintenance men, already investigating a reported leak in the canal, had enough presence of mind to leap clear of the sudden deluge. Even more fortunately, they were able to insert stop planks into narrows built during the second world war in case of bomb damage, so confining the effect of the breach to one instead of seventeen miles.

Of course, in those days - especially 'Up North' - folk made their own entertainment, and the breach was big news. Four policemen were put on special duty to control the excited crowds. People poured in from all over the West Riding almost as rapidly as the water had poured out of the canal. Ten 'expert puddlers' were sent over from Wigan to reline the canal bed. They must have walked straight out of a Monty Python sketch. Ten clones in hobnail boots and braces elbowing their way like gladiators through the hushed throng - "It's t'puddlers!" - and proceeding to go about their routine like a Morris dance in slow motion amidst spontaneous outbursts of applause from a crowd hardly able to contain themselves. Ecky thump!

Scratch the past and see what happens. Like the Leeds & Liverpool itself, the magic is never very far from the surface. Look closely at the corner of the wooden warehouse by Bridge 197, and you will find flyboat semaphore signals (tucked away in the down position) which once were used to convey messages to the passing boatmen of non-stop boats during the heyday of traffic over the canal, when Foulridge to Stockbridge was considered a good day's work for a boat horse. In pleasure-boating terms, the mind baulks at coming to terms with such distances.

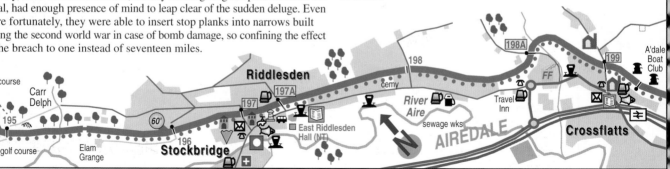

By-road to Keighley (1 mile)   A650 to Keighley SKIPTON

Bingley 3 Rise, Leeds & Liverpool Canal

THE civilised world is divided into those who know Bingley as a centre of thermal underwear manufacture, and those who recognise it as the location of one of the Seven Wonders of the Waterways, the gargantuan BINGLEY FIVE RISE staircase locks. You know, of course, where our interests lie. Yes, that's right, just look at the lacework on that plunge neckline, darling!

The Leeds & Liverpool goes in for a fair amount of plunging too. It plunges down the 5 Rise, it plunges down the 3 Rise; and you too can plunge, metaphorically, into the clam chowder-like waters of the West Riding, a landscape as warmfully, playfully hugging as the latest little number from Damart.

But you'll be wanting some facts, and the facts are that the 5 Rise changes the level of the canal by some sixty vertiginous feet, a thrombotic experience which the canal takes more or less in its stride, even if it leaves most canal users reeling. The staircase has stood its ground since 1774 and must be credited to John Longbotham, the L&L's chief engineer.

Two centuries later it's the pride and joy of its resident lock-keeper,

Barry Whitelock, an appropriately surnamed man who reminds you forcibly of Brian Clough in his pomp at Derby County, and who has a way of treating boat crews and onlookers (of which there are often hundreds at a time) as if they were taking part in one of Cloughie's training sessions all those years ago.

Most of the time Barry will supervise passage through the 5 Rise, working most of the complex paddle gear himself whilst keeping a paternal eye on the proceedings. We hit the locks, however, on the first busy Saturday of the season, and he was called away to assist a wideboat down the 3 Rise, leaving us, effectively, to operate the last four chambers of the 5 Rise for ourselves. It felt a little bit like turning up at the airport and having the pilot ask if we'd mind awfully taxi-ing out on to the runway while he nipped off for a newspaper.

It was worth the licence fee.
Adrenalin-pumping,
we progressed
from one cavernous
chamber to the
next like

Key
1 miscellaneous mills
2 Damart Works
3 Salts Mills
4 Orbic Works
5 Airedale Mills
6 Junction Mills

Hainsworth's Boatyard

15

BINGLEY 5 RISE
No.s 25-29
60ft 0ins
lock-keeper

200
5

A650 from Keighley SKIPTON

1 Bingley
201 3 Rise
No.s 22-24
30ft 0ins
202 60'
Spar

A650 from Harden

B6429 from Harden

203
Safeway

Bingley
park

N

River
Aire

school

FF

Dowley Gap
2 Rise
No.s 20 & 21
18ft 4ins

204

205
26
206
lock-keeper

aqueduct

River
Aire

Hirst Lock
No.19 10ft 2ins

207

60'

ILKLEY   A6038 from Otley

Baildon

Shipley Glen
Tramway

park 207A
3

Saltaire
wc p

former
canal
warehouses

Saltaire

3 Salts

4

207E
207B 207C

207D
6 209
5
208
60'

209A

210 60'

McDonalds
Aldi

Shipley

course of
Bradford
Canal

FF

A650 to Bradford   A650 to Keighley   Bradford city centre 3 miles

Bingley 5 Rise, Leeds & Liverpool Canal

seasoned bargees, playing to the gallery of assembled onlookers.

Set on a bend overlooked by Damart's huge mill, the 3 Rise is scarcely less intimidating, but by now we were old hands. Between the bottom chamber and bridge 202 the canal has been diverted to accommodate a new road which slices Bingley in half with the indifference of a bored chef.

Shaking off high-rise suburbs, the canal proceeds through the glacial moraines of Dowley Gap. Bridge 204 carries the pipework of Bradford Corporation's Nidd Aqueduct water supply channel. DOWLEY GAP 2 RISE lies alongside a sizeable sewage works, but the resident lock-keeper turns his back and regularly wins prizes for the loveliness of his locks, and with the Fisherman's Inn (Tel: 01274 564238), adjacent to nearby Scourer Bridge (205), this is a pleasant and reputedly secure spot to moor overnight. A seven-arch aqueduct spans a reach of the Aire used by the rowing fraternity before the canal enjoys a woodland interlude to the north of HIRST LOCK, where there is an interesting little gathering of old mill buildings.

SALTAIRE holds a unique place on the canal system. Alright, the Worcester & Birmingham skims through Bournville, but there is barely any hint of the model worker's village beyond the towpath, whilst Port Sunlight and New Lanark have no canals at all. And so Saltaire deserves to be savoured, as perhaps Sir Titus always intended: its canyon of fudge-coloured mills, elegant Congregational church and streets of dignified worker's housing named after Titus Salt's children. Moor here, or detour from the towpath, and stroll across the Aire to the Shipley Glen Tramway, a weird Victorian cable incline conveying open carriages up and down through a wooded hillside.

Unlike Saltaire, SHIPLEY has few pretentions to architectural style, though its massive canal warehouses create a distinct impression by virtue of their size alone. Once they would have been stuffed to the gills with angora fleeces. Now they are being refurbished. Their simple dignity contrasts with futuristic office blocks strung along the opposite bank of the canal. Architecture oscillating between the centuries. But it's 'no contest' really, and it takes the unselfconscious functionalism of premises by the electrified swing bridge 209 to provide a favourable effect at the end of the 20th century.

Junction Mills recall the former egress, by bridge 208, of the Bradford Canal, once described as "a seething cauldron of impurity." It was apparently so polluted by the waste from mills and dyeworks as to burn with a blue gas flame. It was abandoned in 1922. Shipley railway station has an unusual triangular layout. Stroll up its still cobbled approach road and treat yourself to a short excursion by electric train to Ilkley or Bradford.

EACH succeeding era of transport has more effrontery than the last. The new Airedale relief road blitzkriegs its way through Bingley impervious to the finer feelings of anything in its path. Similarly, the railway builders of the mid nineteenth century had no qualms about tunnelling under The Nosegay. But the hesitant 18th century canal builders, aware of their engineering inexperience, chose to follow the Aire Valley. Their hesitancy is our gain, for the canal's course is prettily wooded and not at all compromised by the proximity of Bradford Corporation's huge sewage works at Esholt, so extensive that it once boasted its own network of railway lines shunted with steam locomotives fuelled by the waste oils from wool. By swing bridge 211B the main part of the works - imposingly built in hefty stone with liberal scrollwork and coats of arms - was served by a basin which remains in water, if not in use;

though barges were still carrying effluent from Esholt to Knostrop, south of Leeds, at the beginning of the 1980s. A high security fence protects the plant from the attentions of sewage enthusiasts, who might otherwise force an entry and make off with lumps of the stuff as souvenirs. Not readily visible from the canal, Esholt village doubles as *Emmerdale*, Yorkshire Television's soap opera of everyday farming folk. Would be pilgrims may reach it on foot from Bridge 211 in approximately twenty minutes.

DOBSON LOCKS, a 2 Rise, lie alongside a British Waterways yard. Strange to think that all those miles of canal between Greenberfield and Leeds are maintained from this modest collection of workshops and canal workers' cottages. It is no secret, however, that British Waterways derive much of their present income from property deals, a facet of their business demonstrated by the "Moorings" develop-ment at Apperley Bridge. The stone built houses, congregating around a newly dug basin, are pleasing to the eye and harmonise well with the adjoining textile mill erected in 1896.

The canal curves endearingly around the perimeter of Calverley Wood where old quarry faces once provided work for barges. Woodhouse Grove School's playing fields run down to the banks of the Aire.

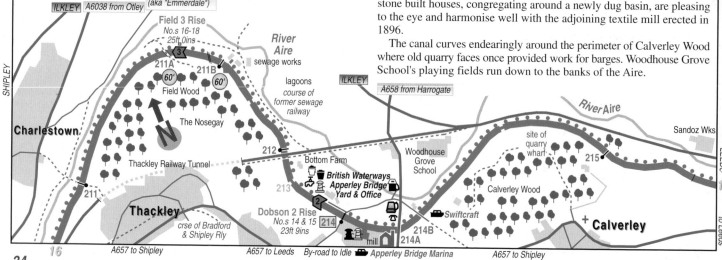

REMINDING one more of the Worcester & Birmingham's approach to Birmingham than the Bridgewater's entrance into Manchester, the Leeds & Liverpool Canal wears its green heart on its sleeve as it winds through the leafy suburbs of Rodley, Newlay and past the rhubarb fields of Kirkstall. The canal builders had no ambitions beyond following the Aire. Perhaps, had it not been so mercurial a watercourse, they might have considered making it navigable. But after a day or two of rain in the Dales, the river's current sweeps all before it, illustrating exactly why it would have been pretty much impractical to use it as the basis of a navigation. The suburbs are 19th and 20th century phenomenons. In the 18th century Airedale was a virtual arcady. Artists as famous as Turner were attracted by its romantic melancholy, especially Kirkstall Abbey. Despite the prevalence of so much greenery, there are outbreaks of industry worth looking out for.

A crane-making works was established at RODLEY in 1820. Here they built plant for some of the world's most prestigious civil engineering projects,

from the Aswan Dam to the Manchester Ship Canal. Peaceful moorings are to be had in Rodley. The Railway (Tel: 0113 257 6603) can be recommended and there's a good fish & chip shop as well. Aire Vale Dyeworks date from 1877, whilst by Bridge 222, the former Kirkstall Brewery has been converted to provide accommodation for Leeds Metropolitan University students. At one time the canal played an important role in transporting the brewery's output. Hogsheads of beer were taken by barge to Goole and transhipped for export on to the brewery's own steamships which traded as far afield as the Antipodes. Nowadays the trade is reversed, and we must put up with "Castlemaine XXXX". But perhaps the most significant industrial activity in this part of the Aire Valley is Kirkstall Forge, where the drop-hammers still thump through each working day as they have done since the 17th century. Nowadays the forge specialises in the production of axles for road vehicles.

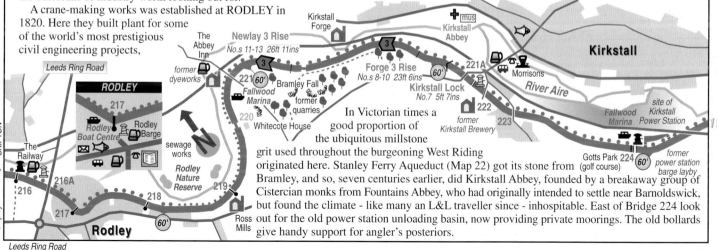

In Victorian times a good proportion of the ubiquitous millstone grit used throughout the burgeoning West Riding originated here. Stanley Ferry Aqueduct (Map 22) got its stone from Bramley, and so, seven centuries earlier, did Kirkstall Abbey, founded by a breakaway group of Cistercian monks from Fountains Abbey, who had originally intended to settle near Barnoldswick, but found the climate - like many an L&L traveller since - inhospitable. East of Bridge 224 look out for the old power station unloading basin, now providing private moorings. The old bollards give handy support for angler's posteriors.

LEEDS, a milestone in any journey: whether it be the last, northern rites of the M1, a hiatus of concrete amongst the terraced houses and lock-up workshops of Holbeck; as a launch pad for the majestic Midland Railway's line to Scotland, alias the Settle & Carlisle; or, in this case, a change of gauge, on what could be a 'Voyage Between Two Seas.' When Pete Morgan arrived here in 1982, to film his so-named journey from the Mersey to the mouth of the Humber for a much-loved BBC television series, he met with Joe Bridge, holder of the unofficial 'Blue Riband' for the canal journey from Liverpool to Leeds. In 1944 he had skippered a horse-drawn cargo of sugar from Tate & Lyle's Liverpool works to Leeds Basin in 52 hours.

Most traffic in the canal was less long distance in character. The major user at this end was Leeds Corporation's Electricity Department who opened a spanking new power station at Kirkstall in 1931 and fed its furnaces with coal brought in by convoys of barges from the Wakefield and Castleford coalfields. Electricity was also generated at a city centre plant on Whitehall Road, which barges reached through a now vanished lock down into the Aire located in the bowels of City railway station. Nowadays, these bowels, or "Dark Arches", liberally doused with Epsom Salts, look very well indeed, having been transformed from gloomy catacombs into the Granary Wharf, a centre for specialist craft shops and small businesses. But in some respects Leeds lags behind the likes of Manchester and Birmingham in the revitalisation of its canal basin, seemingly content to use it as a car park, though refurbishment of the fine stone warehouse alongside River Lock - the formal boundary between the Leeds & Liverpool Canal and the Aire Navigation - as a restaurant and offices, will hopefully have a knock-on effect. Surely the basin could realise more income for its owners as a prime site for property speculation, than as a car park.

Travelling into, or out of, Leeds by canal exposes one to a succulent slice of the city's industrial heritage, the history of which is neatly encapsulated by the displays and artefacts

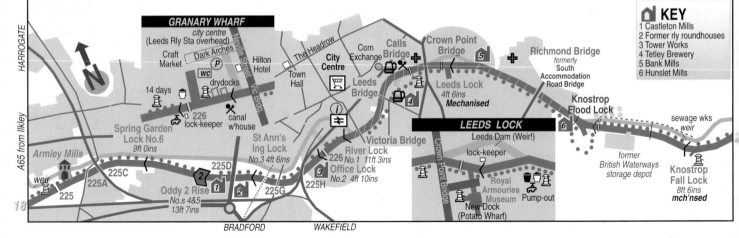

KEY
1 Castleton Mills
2 Former rly roundhouses
3 Tower Works
4 Tetley Brewery
5 Bank Mills
6 Hunslet Mills

Knostrop Flood Lock, Leeds

splendidly housed within the museum at ARMLEY MILLS. Here you can learn how the L&L played a significant role in the transformation of Leeds from a modest wool town into England's third largest city, then step outside on to the towpath and encounter a good many of the cast of that metamorphosis in the flesh, or rather in brick and mortar and millstone grit. Highlights of the journey between Armley Mills and River Lock include: the viaduct which carries the Harrogate line over the Aire Valley at bridge 225C; the sites of Leeds Forge (which once built high pressure boilers for the Royal Navy and rolling stock underframes for the Empire's railway systems) and Leeds's formerly intensive tanning industry; the handsome Castleton Mill built in 1838 for the weaving of flax; the Leeds & Thirsk Railway's round-houses by bridge 225D; and the extraordinary Tower Works looming over OFFICE LOCK, its chimneys heavily disguised as campaniles. Inside, the workforce were not, as you might expect, busily churning out operatic arias, but engaged in the slightly more mundane pastime of manufacturing pins and combs for the wool trade. Those Victorians and their architectural hang-ups! Moor here overnight and you are apt to wake up drowsily imagining that you've floated on to Florence or Verona, until the rumble of the seven-twelve to Huddersfield brings you back to the West Riding with a bump.

The Aire & Calder Navigation

If Granary Wharf lacks a little revivalist zeal, the city's riverfront makes bounteous amends. If there is a more fascinating, adrenalin-pumping urban navigation in the country - Westminster and the Thames notwithstanding - it does not spring readily to mind. We may have been bowled over by the crisp autumnal light illuminating the old warehouses and their modern imposters on the day we made our initial reconnaissance for this guide. And yes, alright, under a sullen Pennine sky it may look all somewhat less prepossessing. But first impressions of places, like people, are difficult to shake off. VICTORIA BRIDGE was designed by George Leather jnr, the Aire & Calder's engineer. Opened in 1839, it replaced an earlier structure swept away by floodwaters. The current can still be capricious, and boaters are advised not to pass down through River Lock if the gauge at the tail of the lock shows only red. Go and watch the current coursing through the Dark Arches and you will see how volatile the Aire can be. But it was made navigable up to Leeds as early as 1700, bringing in its wake, a camp following of mills, warehouses and wharves, so intimate with each other as to create an orgy of industrial premises with the river winding through it. Old engravings, oil paintings and photographs reveal a waterway crowded with vessels like any ring-road at rush hour. Though unlike any ring-road at rush hour, the effect is visually satisfying, even if the river was, by all accounts horribly polluted in the heyday of the water trade. The riverside buildings span the centuries, from 19th century brick warehouses to the futuristic glass and concrete of Tetley's Brewery Wharf, a shortlived, and now forlornly empty, tourist attraction. Where refurbishment has not been practical, new buildings, like the ASDA supermarket chain's head office, have been erected in pleasing harmony.

LEEDS BRIDGE dates from 1873, though there had been a succession of earlier structures at this point since the original ferry was replaced late in the 14th century. It was cast at Butlers Ironworks, Stanningley and has a span of 102ft 6ins. On the south bank, east of the bridge, stand the remnants of the Aire & Calder Navigation's once extensive warehouses which included a covered dock now partially retained as a water feature for a development of modern housing. The company's palatial offices fronting the corner of Dock Street, recently abandoned by British Waterways, are being converted into flats. But it is the presently empty building adjoining the bridge which has the most interesting story - or rather, two stories - to tell. Two plaques above the parapet reveal that the teetotal Band of Hope was founded in this building in 1847, and that the first moving pictures taken with a single lens camera were made from an upstairs window by Louis le Prince forty-one years later. Downstream, you float down the Aire under the gothic gaze of Leeds Parish Church and wine bar balconies to CALLS BRIDGE, a modern footbridge opened in

1993 to improve access between either bank of the revitalised river. The opportunity to moor is here, as long as you remember to leave sufficient slack for any change which might occur in the river level while you're absent. We left the boat, walked with the spirits of long departed boatmen along still-cobbled Dock Street, and lunched at "The Adelphi" amidst flamboyant Edwardian decor that the Aire & Calder's directors may well have been familiar with.

Tetley's Brewery overlooks the reach leading down to CROWN POINT BRIDGE, erected in 1842 to the designs of the Leathers, father and son. Immediately downstream of the bridge the navigation channel proceeds through an artificial cut avoiding the large weir at Leeds Dam. The cut also provides access to New (or Clarence) Dock, nicknamed 'Tattie Dock' by working boatmen due to the preponderance of potato cargoes. Now this sizeable dock is incorporated in the prestigious Royal Armouries Museum development.

Hunslet Mills, stand gloomily derelict, though protected as a listed building. It was built in 1838 as a flax mill, but in latter years was used for the manufacture of blankets. The Aire splits into three channels: the westernmost arm being the river's original course. The eastern channel was cut at the turn of the century to by-pass the old river, whilst, disconcertingly narrow, the centre route is the navigable one, squeezing through the paired gates of KNOSTROP FLOOD LOCK; not really a 'lock' at all, but a pair of mitred gates left open unless there is heavy flooding. South of the floodgates, British Waterways 1958 freight depot, designed to speed up the transit of goods between water and road, has metaphorically turned its back on the navigation, as if saying: "Bollards to barges."

At KNOSTROP FALL LOCK old piers are all that survive of the gargantuan Hunslet Railway swingbridge erected, late in the 19th century, to carry goods trains around the edge of the city at a time when consideration was being given to conversion of the Aire & Calder into a ship canal capable of handling tall-masted sea-going vessels. Local lore has it that the bridge swung only once - on the day it was tested!

 One or two sections of towpath are absent between Granary Wharf and Crown Point Bridge. Follow the blue dots indicated on the map between Victoria Bridge via Leeds Bridge and Dock Road to Calls Bridge.

The
AIRE & CALDER
Navigation

HULL.

39

*I*NDUSTRY has raped and ransacked the Aire Valley's landscape south-east of Leeds. But what do you expect, wasn't the A&C asking for it? The sadness is, that it all couldn't be done with the dignity of Thwaite Mills, as opposed to the smash & grab techniques of opencast mining. For throughout much of this section the countryside resembles a First World War battlefield. Airedale transmogrified into Passchendaele. Though like all battlefields after the battle it is haunted by a strange tranquillity, a *genius loci* of lost causes and pyrrhic victories, a landscape at peace with itself once more.

The Aire was powering a fulling mill at Thwaite in the 17th century, but the gorgeous grouping of almost orange brick buildings, apparently haphazardly laid out upon the isthmus between the canal and river now, date from the first quarter of the 19th century. Down the years the mill has crushed seed to make oil, ground flint for pottery, and chalk to turn into putty. Then, following an enforced retirement brought about by flood damage in 1976, it became a working museum. Skelton Grange power station has been demolished, but you can still see the lay-by where the discharging of coal barges took place.

The towpath is part of the Trans-Pennine Trail. On the far side of the valley, the massive Tudor-Jacobean facade of Temple Newsam Hall attempts, phlegmatically, to ignore the damage eked out on this once serene landscape, whilst FISHPOND LOCK flippantly evokes a level of monastic charm with which reality can no longer equate. Isolated between latent banks of mining spoil, the lock-keeper's only link with the outside world was a miry track connected umbilically with the former mining village of John O' Gaunts.

There are long stay moorings at WOODLESFORD LOCK, picnic tables and a bird hide overlooking the Aire and adjoining mining flashes. Visitor Moorings are provided by Swillington Bridge. Bentley's Yorkshire Brewery used to stand between the canal and the railway, until it fell into the acquisitive hands of Whitbread who, true to their track record, shut it down; now it's a housing development! Alcoholic beverage making survives in the district, however, in the somewhat unlikely guise of what is claimed to be England's most northerly commercial vineyard, located across the Aire at Leventhorpe.

At FLEET BRIDGE there used to be a lock down into the Aire. It was retained so that barges could reach Fleet Mills, long ago demolished. It's heartening to see that the oil depot receives deliveries by barge.

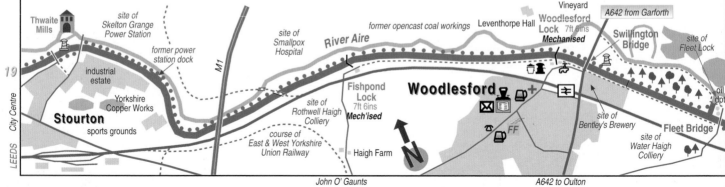

CASTLEFORD

WHY are Castleford's maidens so fair? Because they bathe in the Calder and dry in the Aire. Charming but misrepresentative doggerel: for when we got to the confluence of the Calder with the Aire, there were no bathing beauties, only a chemical plant and a set of traffic lights governing movements to and from the main line of the Aire & Calder Navigation and its Wakefield Branch.

Between Woodlesford and Castleford the Aire has altered its course almost as often as the *Starship Enterprise*,

site of colliery

Allerton Bywater

Lock Lane

Ledston Ings

Aire & Calder to Goole

River Aire

Bulholme Lock
8ft 3ins
Mechanised
chem. wks.

BW

WC & PO

lock-keeper

site of pottery

former coal staithe

River Aire

The Boat

site of ferry

St Aidan's Opencast Mine

site of Kippax Lock

Mickleton Ings

Cawood-Hargreaves

Traffic Lights

Castleford Flood Lock

WEIR

Castleford Bridge

Allinsons Flour Mill

Town Centre

Castleford

chemical works

"The Island"

Lemonroyd Basin

site of Lemonroyd Lock

Coney Moor

Mickletown

Methley Mires

River Calder

site of glass bottle wks
site of Mere Brewery

footbridge

site of Savile Coly Basin

footbridge

gravel pit

Methley Bridge

FF

Lemonroyd Lock 13ft 6ins
Mechanised

l.c.

Methley

Methley Junction

sewage wks

viaduct

Stephenson's Bridge

most recently in the wake of a massive breach which flooded the adjoining opencast coal workings. So valuable is the coal, however, that British Coal - as one of its last pre-privatisation gestures - footed the £20 million bill for a new alignment to be dug combining the river and canal into one navigable channel between Fleet and Kippax. Built by McAlpine's, who apparently approached the job as if they were building a motorway, then simply filled it with water, the new line negotiates a deep lock at Lemonroyd. Engineered on a European scale, you could be making your way between the Rhine and the Danube. Certainly it had been a project, we realised, slightly beyond the scope of our old chums the ten expert puddlers from Wigan.

The towpath peters out at the site of Allerton Bywater ferry. Through walkers or cyclists will need to detour onto footpaths following the northern bank of the navigation.

Provision of a spanking

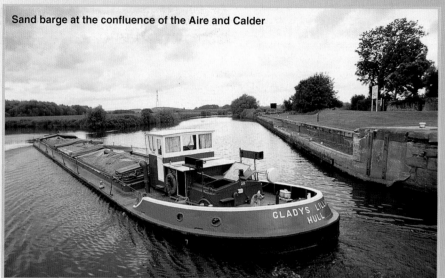

Sand barge at the confluence of the Aire and Calder

as a boater, you intend to stop-over in Castleford, you should pass through the Flood Lock to the Visitor Moorings beyond. East of Castleford the Aire & Calder proceeds through Knottingley (where there is a junction with a navigable section of the River Aire leading to the Selby Canal) to Goole and the tidal Ouse. There is also a connection, by way of the New Junction Canal, with the South Yorkshire Navigation to Sheffield.

But in this guide, we're heading west out of Castleford along the

new staithe at St Aidans temporarily enabled opencast coal to be taken down to Ferrybridge power station by push-tows. But this has been consigned to recent history too, vanishing almost as abruptly as it was built. Allerton Bywater Colliery was the last deep mine in the district. It closed in March 1992. 'Tom Puddings' loaded coal here for export from Goole where each compartment was levitated by means of a massive coal hoist and its contents tipped into the holds of sea-going colliers. This, in the days when Britain was an exporter, rather than an importer, of coal. Two huge, corrugated-iron clad loading shutes stood waterside where now only some masonry banking remains, and the only vessels likely to tie-up here are pleasure craft whose occupants fancy a quiet pint at "The Boat", a convivial home brew pub.

CASTLEFORD has always been a waterway crossroads. The Flood Lock is usually open unless there are excess currents in the rivers, and if,

Aire & Calder's Wakefield Branch to join the Calder & Hebble. Between Castleford and Woodnook (Map 22) the navigation traverses a flat landscape occluded by high banks in a manner reminiscent of The Fens. 'Caz' lies hunched across the horizon like someone slumped over a bar. Power lines festoon the fields, glassily reflected in isolated oxbow meanders of the Calder's old course. One of these remained navigable for many years to reach a bottle factory, brewery and pottery works. In the rheumy distance, Ferrybridge's cooling towers foam at the mouth, whilst beyond Allerton Bywater the gracious facade of Ledston Hall reminds one that there was a degree of pre-industrial grace in the vicinity. Two interesting railway viaducts span the river. The easternmost, now trackless, carried the Lancashire & Yorkshire Railway's route between Pontefract and Leeds; the westernmost, still in use, the North Eastern Railway's line from Castleford to Leeds.

BLACK fades to green as abandoned coal workings are reclaimed, returning Caldervale to its pastoral origins; though the creation of the Wakefield Europort logistics centre has somewhat reversed this process. When the Castleford & Wakefield Cut was opened in 1839 it almost halved the distance by water between the two towns. Much junketing took place at STANLEY FERRY where the old, sinuous course of the Calder was spanned by an elegant aqueduct, an iron trough suspended between bow-spring girders with classical ornamentations at either end; an elopement of 19th century England with Ancient Greece which is said to have spawned the Sydney Harbour Bridge. Had the aqueduct been in Warwickshire or Northamptonshire or some such county where canals have achieved cult status, it would have been better known. No one paid the structure much attention until British Waterways decided to retire it, by-passing it with a concrete aqueduct itself the victim of a charisma by-pass. The old aqueduct, they said, wasn't up to taking the strain of modern commercial traffic. But, as is so often the ironic way of things, hardly had the new aqueduct opened when trade all but vanished.

Three boater-operated automated locks punctuate the boater's progress east of Stanley Ferry. The BW key accessed, push-button controls are reputedly foolproof, but we miss the keepers who were still here when we researched the first edition of this guide back in 1995. One valued their good humour, their common sense, and the way they called you 'cock' with an easy familiarity suggesting you were just about to go whippet racing together. Local boaters

Kirkthorpe

The Half Moon

site of former lock

23

Broadreach Flood Lock

Harrison's Bridge

site of Park Hill Colliery

Welbeck Land Reclamation Site

course of min rly

Ramsden's Swing Bridge aqueducts

Birkwood Farm

STANLEY FERRY

new aq.

Mill House

old aq.

Ship Inn

BW

M62 Eastbound / WAKEFIELD

Bridge Inn

golf course

EWS depot

Whitwood Wharf

Fairies Hill Lock

viaduct

Wakefield Europort

By-road from Altofts (pub, shop, fish & chips)

Kings Road Lock 7ft 0ins *Mechanised*

Birkwood Lock 7ft 0ins *Mechanised*

viaduct

site of Altofts Lock

Royal Mail depot

ASDA depot

site of Foxholes Lock

site of Bottomboat staithe

Woodnook Lock 13ft 6ins *Mechanised*

Pennbank Farm

weir

River Calder

Lake Lock *former A&C maint yrd*

course of LMS & LNER Joint Rly

21

CASTLEFORD

N

M62 Westbound

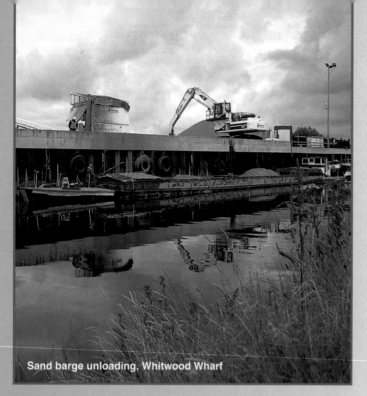

Sand barge unloading, Whitwood Wharf

quarries on the River Trent. It would probably be stretching credibility too far to expect the neighbouring postal and supermarket warehouses to follow in Lafarge's footsteps, but there might well be other businesses located in the Europort who would benefit from water transport.

Elsewhere, the canal traverses a lonely, inaccessible, surprisingly agricultural tract of land. Pylons plod across the fields emphasising the efficacy of cramming one's portfolio with electricity shares, just as in the past it paid dividends to invest in the Aire & Calder who, faced with the onset of railway competition, kept abreast of engineering progress by constructing 'cuts' to shorten the river's meanderings, and gradually increasing the dimensions of the locks to accept ever larger craft. Fairies Hill and Altofts locks were by-passed by a new lock at WOODNOOK. The old lock at Fairies Hill has been retained to provide access to moorings, both overnight and long term. If you're contemplating a stay here overnight you might find the neighbouring Bridge Inn (Tel: 01977 550498) a useful port of call. It can be reached by way of a public footpath skimming a municipal golf course from the aggregates wharf at Whitwood.

The navigation's old line, spanned by a particularly handsome railway viaduct, provides moorings at either end. But despite such improvements, old reaches of the river continued to be navigated where access was still required to established premises. Foxholes Lock facilitated entry to the Aire & Calder Company's extensive workshops at Stanley. Converted into housing these days, they are still visible on the riverbank beneath the village's impressive church. When the old yard closed, new workshops were opened on the site of a former boatbuilding yard at STANLEY FERRY, and for many years this became a maintenance centre for the 'Tom Puddings', the tug-hauled compartment pans invented by William Hammond Bartholomew, the A&C's most illustrious manager, for carrying coal. One of the 'Pudding's' regular sources of coal was from St John's Colliery whose basin lay opposite the yard. At one time the compartments were hoisted individually out of the water and conveyed along a mineral railway for loading at the pit head.

South of Stanley Ferry, the canal runs straight through a shallow cutting, this was the location of Park Hill Colliery and a busy loading staithe abutted the canal. Skipton Gas Works, took its coal from here, as did Kirkstall Power Station.

miss them very much too. The suggestion being that vandalism flourishes in their absence. This is society's problem, not the canals', but it does seem sadly inevitable that hooliganism fills a void almost exponentially.

A welcome boost for water transport is the result of Lafarge's new riverside aggregates wharf at Whitwood. An estimated 25,000 lorries are absent from the road network annually because this far sighted company has taken the trouble to site their depot here and use barges - some of them in their own house colours - to bring materials here from gravel pits and

WAKEFIELD marks the boundary between the Aire & Calder and Calder & Hebble navigations, the actual point of demarcation being FALL ING LOCK. East of here the A&C, criss-crossed by railway lines, curves, otherwise unremarkably, around the periphery of the city, passing the barely detectable, and long defunct, junction of the Barnsley Canal. Officially abandoned in 1953, the canal had enjoyed its best years under the ownership of the Aire & Calder when it was a busy outlet for coal from the many pits in the area. At one time it connected with the Sheffield & South Yorkshire Navigation via the Dearne & Dove Canal, a lost route through the swarthy interior of Barnsley's coalfields, intermittently mourned sufficiently enough for restoration to rear its dubious head. Heath Old Hall looms romantically through the treetops on a wooded bluff above the riverbank. Mooring is problematical, but

walkers can find their way easily enough up on to the neighbouring common, a delightful throwback to pre-industrial Caldervale.

The Aire & Calder's Wakefield terminus lay adjacent to the city's famous chantry bridge chapel, one of only five remaining in Britain, the others being at Rotherham, Bradford-on-Avon, Derby and the Cambridgeshire St Ives, tempting one to devise an inland waterway itinerary visiting all five bridge chapels by boat. Some fascinating old warehouses and offices remain intact around the Aire & Calder's basin but the arm itself is no longer navigable.

A short length of cut - providing useful mooring facilities for Wakefield - separates Fall Ing and Wakefield Flood locks. The latter provides access to (and egress from) a broad reach of the Calder

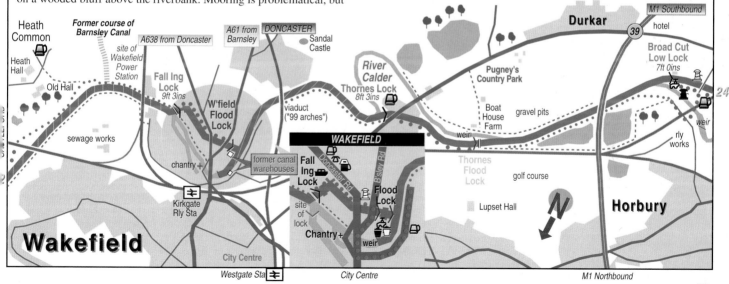

overlooked by some interesting mills and warehouses. Trade here must have been brisk. Boat captains were apparently in the habit of speculating in local property as an investment towards retirement. Two notable riverside industries still in business are the Wakefield Shirt Company (Double Two) and Rawsons Carpets which was still receiving consignments of jute and coir fibre by barge in the mid Seventies. Nearby, modern double-deckers occupy garaging facilities once devoted to the upkeep of Wakefield's trams.

Fall Ing Lock, Wakefield

The main railway route between London and Leeds crosses the Calder upon a cast iron bridge (with battlemented abutments) incorporated into a lengthy viaduct. Locally this is known as the "ninety-nine arches", though some myth-shattering guidebooks would have it that there are only ninety-five. Have they no soul? There are glimpses, upstream, of the motte & bailey remains of Sandal Castle, whilst nearby a housing estate occupies the site of the Battle of Wakefield in 1460, one of the rainbow-coloured reminders that "Richard of York gave battle in vain."

The north bank of the river is given over to rhubarb growing (a local speciality worth looking in to) against a backdrop of Wakefield's skyline, dominated by the soaring spire of the city's cathedral and the high clock-towered town hall.

Thornes Cut eradicates a discursive meander. Once upon a time THORNES LOCK had duplicated chambers. An adjoining wire works featured a large asbestos clad warehouse with a canopy overhanging the river. Barges brought coils of wire here until 1967, but since our last update the works has been demolished and replaced, symbolically, by a health & fitness club and a modern pub and a 'fun factory'. Between THORNES FLOOD LOCK and BROAD CUT LOW LOCK the Calder runs through an area of gravel working and passes beneath the M1 motorway. Elmley Moor's massive transmitting mast - taller than the Eiffel Tower - is a dominant landmark to the south-west. In the old days a ferry carried the boat horses across the Calder at Broad Cut Low Lock. Now walkers are faced with a detour by way of the nearby railway bridge, somewhat un-nervingly provided with a pitch-black walkway sandwiched between the tracks above and the foaming waters of the river below. Having fitted out Virgin's 'Voyager' fleet, the railway works is due to close.

RUNNING to the south of the town of HORBURY, along a five mile section of man-made cut, the Calder & Hebble conveys a surprising sense of isolation, a feeling intensified by the cessation of coal mining in the area. Opening of the cut, piecemeal, eradicated some of the Calder's most extravagant meanderings and lessened delays caused by flooding; though, as we have noted elsewhere, as several industries were already established along the riverbank, some sections of navigation were retained and locks provided through from the new cut to the river. Examples of this are to be seen at HORBURY BRIDGE - where the old connecting basin has been redeveloped as moorings - and at FIGURE OF THREE LOCKS where the abandoned chamber now acts as an overflow weir. The Calder itself has also seen changes to its course, some natural, others, like its realignment to facilitate the construction of Healey Mills marshalling yard, man made. It was the original shape of the river at Healey which gave the locks their unusual name. The Reverend Sabine Baring-Gould, writer of *Onward Christian Soldiers*, had connections with Horbury.

Between BROAD CUT TOP LOCK and Bridge 32 the canal traverses a melancholy girder-spanned, heron-haunted corridor of silver birch and cindery wasteground climaxed by the death knell ruin of the British Oak Colliery loading staithe, last used in 1981, and recently 'tidied-up' and accordingly diminished by purveyors of municipal vandalism. Oh to see again a West Country keel (no clotted cream connotation, but rather the vessels which gravitated towards the *west* of the Humber's working waterways) chugging up the cut laden with coal from British Oak destined for Thornhill Power Station on the far side of Dewsbury. Oh to be in England when it did an honest day's work and was not simply content to be a virtual reality, modem-linked annex of Disneyland.

Virgin fields blanket the site of Hartley Bank Colliery. Some of the bridges retain charming triangular Calder & Hebble number plates. Half urban, half rural, the canal reminded us of the lower echelons of the Caldon Canal where it tries to shake off the shackles of The Potteries. It is at Figure of Three that westbound travellers encounter their first example of the Calder & Hebble's indigenous handspike-worked paddle gear. An initiation ceremony ensues. Men are separated from boys; engineers from poets.

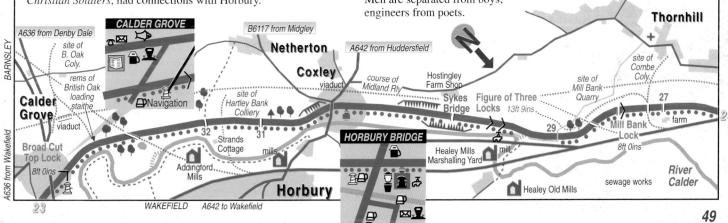

THE deeper the Calder & Hebble journeys up its valley, the more colloquial it becomes. You can almost picture, in all those stern of countenance, millstone grit villas, elderly ladies masticating lemon bonbons and washing out the wrinkles in their support stockings. The Calder & Hebble could do with ironing-out its own wrinkles, needing all the support it can get, for in the Thornhill Cut, together with the river section downstream of Greenwood, it is at its least edifying. Usually only too susceptible to the neo-romantic siren call of post-industrial decay, even we felt disenfranchised by the sheer ugliness of these waters, deeming this stretch as vile as any we had ever come upon on our canal travels; BCN notwithstanding. But perhaps we were tired, or depressed by the weather, or furious with the brambles on the overgrown towpath, or cheated by the absence of orange-coloured Hargreaves keels plying to and from the now obliterated power station wharf at

Thornhill. But that's what you get for using a guidebook notoriously prone to bouts of self-doubt and subjectivity.

The DEWSBURY ARM doesn't take prisoners. Your senses are sent down for assault and battery. Once, prior to construction of the Thornhill Cut, it formed a through route, rejoining the river to the north of its latter-day terminus at Savile Town. It is an unimaginative canal explorer, though, who can resist an arm's temptation. Go on, kill the cat with curiosity, push your prow past the cement works, the steel-holding yards, the scrap yards and the breeze block yards to where the mosques and minarets of downtown Dewsbury look devoutly down upon its boat-filled terminus.

Between Dewsbury and Mirfield the navigation continues to alternate between man-made cuts and river sections, making for fascinating contrasts, especially when boating. Gloomy as the THORNHILL CUT can be, it has its leavening moments: the handsome 1847 cast-iron span of the London & North Western Railway; the Yorkshire Transformer Works, debauched by the decay of its redundantly pretentious concrete architecture; the adjoining

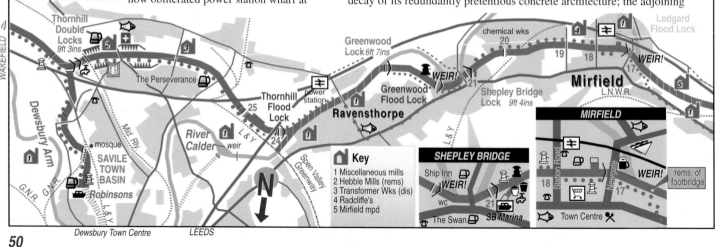

Key
1 Miscellaneous mills
2 Hebble Mills (rems)
3 Transformer Wks (dis)
4 Radcliffe's
5 Mirfield mpd

Dewsbury Town Centre   LEEDS

stone-built warehouse; and the discarded Hebble Mills, reduced to a sequence of high rounded arches like something out of a surrealist painting by Chirico.

Sustrans are reinvigorating the trackbed of the Lancashire & Yorkshire Railway's Spen Valley route. If you're on foot it's worth a detour, if only to pass beneath the London & North Western and cross the Calder to where a four aspect colour light signal has escaped the demolition gangs' attention and now stands as a reminder that trains once went this way.

No other guidebook quite prepares you for the degeneracy of the Calder in the neighbourhood of Ravensthorpe. One of the mills around here became famous for supplying blankets to the Red Indians of North America. Now they probably provide dental floss to the man in the moon. A new gas power station occupies the site of the old coal fired plant at Thornhill. Detritus spills out from riverside factories. A skeletal grey girder bridge spans the water. Morale becomes difficult to sustain.

GREENWOOD CUT breaches the trade descriptions act, being bordered by an industrial estate and sundry wastegrounds. A short curving section of river, with a broad weir, separates it from SHEPLEY BRIDGE. Note how the upstream section of each cut is protected by flood gates, whilst their lower ends feature conventional locks.

At Shepley Bridge an old boatbuilding yard, latterly used by British Waterways, enjoys a new lease of life as a hire base and provider of boating facilities. The MIRFIELD CUT is approximately a mile long. Some characterful properties and premises overlook the canal: saturnine Victorian villas, gaunt mills and (our favourite) the works of Squire A. Radcliffe & Sons, blenders of textile waste oils who occupy maltings separated from the towpath by a still-cobbled road. Mirfield was the birthplace of wooden West Country keels; the last, *Isobel*, being launched in 1955. Sister barge, the *Ethel* is preserved at the Boat Museum, Ellesmere Port. The drydock was originally the route of the navigation prior to opening of the Mirfield Cut.

Two sections of towpath are, to all intents and purposes, non existent, necessitating detours on to adjoining roads between Ravensthorpe and Shepley Bridge and Mirfield and Battyeford (Map 26).

Thornhill Double Locks

RUBBING off on you yet, the Calder & Hebble's elusive charm? Certainly the frequent juxtaposition of river navigation with canal cut keeps the adrenalin - as well as the Calder itself - flowing: in its 22 miles it falls over 190 feet through 27 locks. BATTYEFORD LOCK is overlooked by the "Pear Tree Inn" which has a mooring jetty for boating patrons just upstream from the entrance of the cut. Above the lock, the friendly South Pennine Boat Club occupy the site of a former boatbuilding yard whose drydock survives. On the neighbouring hillside, Mirfield Monastery, occupied by the Order of the Resurrection, stands aloof from the Calder Valley with its pale green rooftops. The church was built between 1910 and 1939 on the site of a former quarry, partially adapted as an open-air theatre. The adjoining house belonged to a family whose fortune was made selling blankets during the Franco-Prussian War. Bedding is still manufactured locally at the Nunbrook Mills overlooking the adjacent weir.

At COOPER BRIDGE the waters of one of the Calder's most significant tributaries, the Colne, make their presence felt amidst a plethora of sewage works. Robin Hood and Little John forded across the Calder hereabouts at the end of their ill-fated journey to Kirklees Priory in 1247, where the hero of Sherwood Forest is said to have been bled to death by the treacherous abbess.

The Colne and the Calder are not the only junction-makers at Cooper Bridge, for the Huddersfield Broad meets the Calder & Hebble here as well - see Map 26A. Islanded between the two navigable waterways stands an interesting collection of wharf buildings overlooked by the high-chimnied mill of the Holme Spinning Company. 'Down South', on a more popular canal, it would make a wonderful base for a craft centre and tea rooms. Collectors of the obscure and enigmatic should stroll down the A643 to its junction with the A62, where the Dumb Steeple, a roadside monument to the efforts of local Luddites to jam the brakes on Progress can be found. By definition, a high proportion of canal travellers will be inclined to wish they had succeeded.

Hidden by woodland, Robin Hood's grave overlooks the KIRKLEES CUT, a refreshingly green interval between the urban impregnations of Cooper Bridge and Brighouse. Kirklees corn mill has been converted into a restaurant, but the unbridged river renders it inaccesible from the canal. Minor details kindle images of the past: a stone distance post marking 100 yards to the Low Lock; a curious horizontal wheel at the tail of Kirklees Lock which presumably had some function to do with the tow-rope of horse-drawn keels; and a Lancashire & Yorkshire Railway boundary stone.

The M62 crosses the cut near its reunion with the river at Anchor Pit. Bumper to bumper, the volume of traffic apparent on its high-stilted crossing of the valley emphasises that the demand for Trans-Pennine trade continues, though it is a long time since this inland waterway was an integral part of the most expeditious method of transferring goods from Lancashire to Yorkshire.

Between Anchor Pit and Brighouse the highest navigable reach of the Calder creeps, somewhat uninspiringly, through a corridor of industrial premises; lucrative, no doubt, but mundane, like the "specialist in reclamation of indexable toolings." Heaven help anyone who gets stuck next to one of their employees at a dinner party. By a bend in the river, two short terraces of stone housing apparently still depend on outside privvies.

BRIGHOUSE is a comely little town, though its waterfront has jettisoned degrees of character with the mothballing of Sugden's massive flour mill; looking more and more surreal each time we pass. Sugden was a local builder of keels before becoming a dusty miller. A Sainsbury supermarket provides practical (if less stimulating, from an industrial archaeological outlook) consolation. The basin rarely lacks interest, being home to a boatbuilder of the leisure age and the permanent moorings of the local boating fraternity.

Wharf buildings, Cooper Bridge

PRE-INDUSTRIALLY, the Calder Valley must have been beguilingly beautiful. Here and there echoes of this long forgotten rustic charm remain intact: a luxuriantly wooded hillside to the north; a sprinkling of farms between the factories. And so all kinds of oddly juxtaposed images catch the eye: beef cattle fattening against a factory wall; a pair of disused lock-keepers offices; sundry distance posts made of stone; a ruined lock connecting with the river; some flooded gravel pits; but most provocatively, a high chimnied salute from the tree-tops

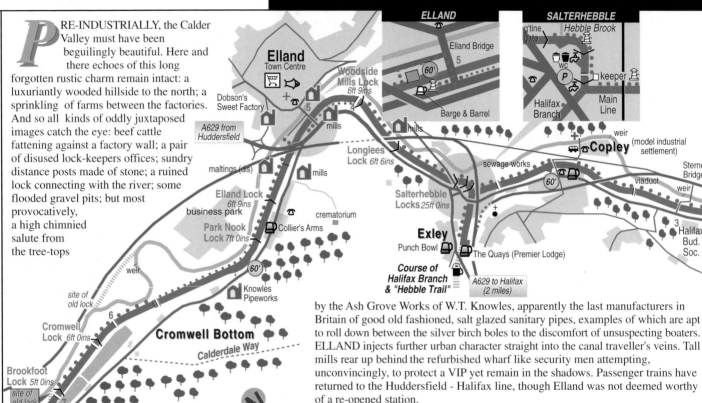

by the Ash Grove Works of W.T. Knowles, apparently the last manufacturers in Britain of good old fashioned, salt glazed sanitary pipes, examples of which are apt to roll down between the silver birch boles to the discomfort of unsuspecting boaters. ELLAND injects further urban character straight into the canal traveller's veins. Tall mills rear up behind the refurbished wharf like security men attempting, unconvincingly, to protect a VIP yet remain in the shadows. Passenger trains have returned to the Huddersfield - Halifax line, though Elland was not deemed worthy of a re-opened station.

The trio of locks at SALTERHEBBLE are arguably the most picturesque and well cared for on the Calder & Hebble. They are laid out around a dog-leg curve. The top two were once a staircase, whilst the bottom lock features an unusual,

Top lock, Salterhebble

town. Even as canals go, it was a heavy drinker. And because the local mills already had the valley's water supplies sewn up, water for the branch was pumped (at the rate of a thousand gallons a minute) up from the main line in an Escher-like arrangement of perpetual motion. Opened in 1828, the Halifax Branch became one of the less publicised abandonments of the LMS Railway's infamous 1944 Act, and much of its course has subsequently been obliterated, though you get some idea of its topography from the right hand side of a slow-climbing train, or more intimately by walking or cycling the "Hebble Trail", an enlivening, traffic-free right of way between the foreshortened terminus of the branch and the centre of Halifax. We were amused to discover that one of the branch's more notable cargoes was 'goux', a euphemism for domestic sewage, exported to the East Riding and Lincolnshire for use as fertilizer. A few hundred yards of the Halifax Branch remains in water at the Salterhebble end, with a bustling modern pub and travel lodge with visitor moorings providing reason enough for a short detour.

Between Salterhebble and Sterne Bridge the canal rides above a valley floor littered with sewage plants and factory premises. The Calder's flanks, however, are sylvan enough to create a favourable impression with those who like their inland waterway journeys on the pretty side. A many arched stone viaduct carries the Manchester-Bradford railway across the Calder & Hebble at Copley, a community based on a model mill village of 19th century worker's housing down by the riverside. Its church stands on the opposite bank, masked by woodland, through which pleasant footpaths run. There is a splendid little cricket ground boxed in by the railways and the river - do they award seven runs if you manage to hit the ball over the viaduct?

A recently demolished mill at Sterne Bridge belonged to the Sterne family of novelist Laurence fame, writer of that rambling 18th century novel "Tristram Shandy". Another literary connection here relates to Wordsworth's poem "Lucy Gray", which was inspired by an incident involving the drowning of a young girl when the bridge was swept away by a winter flood. At the end of the poem, Wordsworth suggests that Lucy Gray is still to be seen: 'smoothly tripping along, singing a solitary song, and whistling in the wind'. Look out for her ...

electrically-operated (out with your sanitary station key) guillotine gate at its tail, an introduction necessitated by widening of the adjacent road bridge. We were interested to see that the gate was manufactured by Ransome & Rapier of Ipswich, a firm perhaps better known, in transport enthusiast circles at least, for their railway turntables. And, yes, we did manage to get it jammed, an embarrassing incident resulting in our wakening of the lock-keeper from his Saturday afternoon snooze. The secret, apparently, is to ensure that the conventional mitred gates at the top of the lock are tightly shut before attempting to operate the guillotine!

In the short pound between the middle and lower locks, a small aqueduct spans the Calder & Hebble's junior partner; a shy, retiring sort of chap called Hebble Brook, who springs to life on t'moors above Halifax. Time was when a branch canal climbed through fourteen locks in less than two miles to reach the centre of that sooty, hill-bounded textile and engineering

REACHING Sowerby Bridge, the Calder & Hebble goes into a telephone box, puts its underpants on outside its trousers, and emerges as the Rochdale Canal, Superman of the inland waterways, fully equipped to take on the tyrannical Pennines. Sowerby basin provides an effective backdrop for this transformation scene. Here, in the early 19th century heyday of Trans-Pennine carriage by water, Mersey Flats exchanged their cargoes with West Country Keels because the Lancashire vessels were, at 70ft long, too large to negotiate the Calder & Hebble's stumpy locks. Such delays did little to help the canals compete with the emerging railways. Trade was abandoned across the summit of the Rochdale Canal before the Second World War, whilst the last waterborne cargo to reach Sowerby Bridge from the east was paper pulp on the keel *Frugality* in September 1955.

Not even a fortune-teller would have dared suggest that, forty years later, the Calder & Hebble and Rochdale canals would be relinked, but that was the almost miraculous turn of events which occured in 1996.

The Calder & Hebble approaches Sowerby Bridge from the east clinging to a shelf above the Calder. Cuddled in shallow hawthorn cuttings, or raised above the river on sapling-framed embankments, the inland waterway traveller's perspective is curtailed, creating a sense of intimacy that intensifies one's relationship with the canal. The hills and mills and railway lines provide reminders of the Upper Peak Forest Canal, but the most spectacular sight on this length is Wainhouse's Tower, an astonishing 253ft high tower of blackened ashlar stone, erected as a chimney for a dyeworks, though never used as such and later converted into a viewing tower. Open to the public on selected dates, 403 steps will take you to the top where, they always said, you could see Blackpool on a clear day, but days were seldom clear in the smoky West Riding of years gone by. In the Twenties it was employed, somewhat bizarrely, as a transmission tower for a local wireless station.

Sowerby Bridge basin retains a good deal of the latent atmosphere of trade. It was here that Dennis Waterman did his best to seduce Jan Francis aboard her residential keel in the

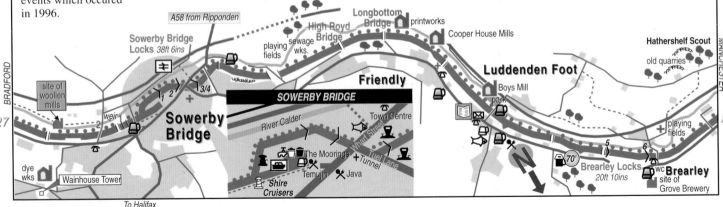

fondly remembered television series *Stay Lucky*. But it is the architecture of the stone warehouses and the boat busy basin - where the Calder & Hebble terminated in 1770 pending the Rochdale's arrival from Lancashire in 1811 - which seduces the rest of us.

The Rochdale Canal swerves past the terminal basin and immediately declares its intention to conquer the Pennines by negotiating a pair of original locks (the first being named after Albert Wood, once the canal's principal trader) followed by one new, and very, very deep lock replacing two earlier chambers. The new lock (whose keeper can be contacted in advance on 01422 316678) was part of the Tuel Lane project reconnecting the Rochdale to the Calder & Hebble following development over the original course of the canal.

Running on a ledge between the river and its steep-sided valley, beneath the engagingly-named suburb of Friendly, the Rochdale enjoys an uncharacteristic paucity of locks, a pound extending to all of two and a half miles, which westbound boaters will grow to cherish with nostalgia and affection. A purer, decanted version of Calderdale seems to accompany the Rochdale as opposed to the Calder & Hebble. The mundane accoutrements of modern Britain are filtered out by the encroaching valley slopes, as if a darker, almost necromantic enchantment is hidden in these folds of millstone grit. Branwell Bronte, the literary sister's ne'er-do-well brother, was briefly station clerk at LUDDENDEN FOOT, and must have been familiar with, if hardly a habitue of, the gaunt, clock-towered United Reform Church overlooking the canal by Cooper House Mills, and with barges loading at the handsome, four-storey stone warehouse occupied by a camping gear stockist overlooking Boys Park. The past may well, as L.P. Hartley put it, be a 'foreign country', but there are cheap package tours departing daily, if you have the imagination to join them.

BREARLEY LOCKS lie in an attractive setting overlooked by woods and adjacent to an ancient stone bridge spanning the Calder. The lower lock is called Edward Kilner after one of the company's engineers. Rochdale locks were 'standardised', as far as feasible, at between nine and ten feet rise so as to simplify the construction of gates and permit them to be interchangable. Follow the lane across the river, past another sizeable, if less ostentatious and now secularly used, chapel, and

public footpaths will take you up on to the quarried face of Hathershelf Scout. Indeed, a good deal of the charm of a boating trip along the heavily-locked Rochdale Canal, lies with the opportunity, every now and then, for you to moor and rest your paddle-gear-weary muscles and walk up on to the neighbouring ridges. Up there the world - or at least this part of the mid-Pennines - is your oyster, and the views can be intoxicating. There was once a brewery at Brearley, presumably a customer of the canal's barges. It's long gone, but you can console yourself with a visit to the Grove Inn by Brearley Locks - Tel: 01422 844650.

Playing fields border the canal on the outskirts of MYTHOLMROYD as the Calder slips unnoticed behind an estate of industrial units. Its name means 'river of stones or hard water', and it makes a journey of over fifty miles from its source above Todmorden to its confluence with the Aire at Castleford.

The Rochdale Canal, Sowerby Bridge

The ROCHDALE Canal

29 ROCHDALE CANAL

CALDERDALE narrows in a westerly direction like a duck decoy. Railway, road, canal and river are packed evermore tightly together as if they were a quartet of buxom farmwives on the back seat of a market day bus. MYTHOLMROYD has connections with the poet Ted Hughes and the 18th century 'coiners' who operated a counterfeit mint in this inaccessible moorland location. In 1956 a pair of gorillas escaped from a private zoo in the neighbourhood. Occasional sightings suggest that some of their offspring live wild in the hills above Calderdale. Apparently, their natural reaction when encountering humans is to remain motionless. It's doubtful if they'd ever be seen beside the canal, but should you do so, please respect their dignity.

HEBDEN BRIDGE embraces the canal with an uncharacteristic show of emotion by West Riding standards. Prodigal sons returning to these parts are expected to supply their own fatted calves. But Calderdale folk seem genuinely pleased to have a navigable canal back in their midst. The setting could hardly be bettered. With a backdrop of the town's leap-frogging buildings, the twin-armed and cobbled wharf is followed, to the west, by a lock, then a low, four arch aqueduct across the Calder adjacent to its confluence with the Hebden Water.

Stephenson's Manchester & Leeds Railway crosses the canal at CHARLESTOWN. West of here the canal becomes more introverted: wizened trees waltz down to its southern bank. The Calder, coursing over its rocky bed is hard to equate with its navigable status below Brighouse. Wildernesses of peat bogs and moss are up there unseen, shadowing your progress along the valley's gutter-like floor.

59

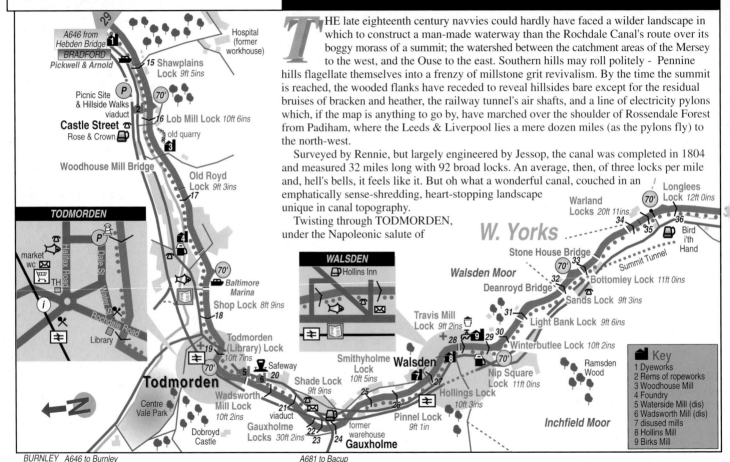

THE late eighteenth century navvies could hardly have faced a wilder landscape in which to construct a man-made waterway than the Rochdale Canal's route over its boggy morass of a summit; the watershed between the catchment areas of the Mersey to the west, and the Ouse to the east. Southern hills may roll politely - Pennine hills flagellate themselves into a frenzy of millstone grit revivalism. By the time the summit is reached, the wooded flanks have receded to reveal hillsides bare except for the residual bruises of bracken and heather, the railway tunnel's air shafts, and a line of electricity pylons which, if the map is anything to go by, have marched over the shoulder of Rossendale Forest from Padiham, where the Leeds & Liverpool lies a mere dozen miles (as the pylons fly) to the north-west.

Surveyed by Rennie, but largely engineered by Jessop, the canal was completed in 1804 and measured 32 miles long with 92 broad locks. An average, then, of three locks per mile and, hell's bells, it feels like it. But oh what a wonderful canal, couched in an emphatically sense-shredding, heart-stopping landscape unique in canal topography.

Twisting through TODMORDEN, under the Napoleonic salute of

Map labels:

A646 from Hebden Bridge
BRADFORD
Pickwell & Arnold
Hospital (former workhouse)
15 Shawplains Lock 9ft 5ins
Picnic Site & Hillside Walks viaduct
Castle Street
Rose & Crown
16 Lob Mill Lock 10ft 6ins
old quarry
Woodhouse Mill Bridge
Old Royd Lock 9ft 3ins
17

TODMORDEN
market
wc
TH
i
Halifax Road
Dale St
Water St
Rochdale Road
Library
4
Baltimore Marina
Shop Lock 8ft 9ins
18
Todmorden (Library) Lock 10ft 7ins
19
Todmorden
Safeway
20
Shade Lock 9ft 9ins
5
6
Wadsworth Mill Lock 10ft 2ins
21
viaduct
Centre Vale Park
Dobroyd Castle
Gauxholme Locks 30ft 2ins
22
23
24
Gauxholme
former warehouse

WALSDEN
Hollins Inn
Travis Mill Lock 9ft 2ins
Smithyholme Lock 10ft 5ins
Walsden
7
8
9
28
29
30
31
Nip Square Lock 11ft 0ins
25
26
Hollings Lock 10ft 3ins
27
Pinnel Lock 9ft 1in

Longlees Lock 12ft 0ins
70'
Warland Locks 20ft 11ins
34
35
36
Bird i'th Hand
W. Yorks
Stone House Bridge
Summit Tunnel
33
32
Bottomley Lock 11ft 0ins
Walsden Moor
Deanroyd Bridge
Sands Lock 9ft 3ins
Light Bank Lock 9ft 6ins
Winterbutlee Lock 10ft 2ins
Ramsden Wood
Inchfield Moor

BURNLEY A646 to Burnley
A681 to Bacup

Key
1 Dyeworks
2 Rems of ropeworks
3 Woodhouse Mill
4 Foundry
5 Waterside Mill (dis)
6 Wadsworth Mill (dis)
7 disused mills
8 Hollins Mill
9 Birks Mill

Gauxholme Locks, Todmorden

Stoodley Pike, which sits like a rocket about to be launched on the moors, the canal bids hail and farewell to the Calder. Todmorden (or Library) Lock has an electrically operated guillotine gate at its tail, accessed by a BW Watermate key. Twisting past the 'Great Wall of Todmorden' (a massive blue brick retaining wall supporting the adjoining railway) before climbing assiduously through sundry settlements of herring-bone-terraced housing and fish-scale-coloured weaving sheds. This is the twenty-first century for goodness sake, but in Gauxholme and Walsden it might still be the eighteenth. Cobbled alleys support washing lines. Heathery banks, in the process of being rapidly colonised by rhododendrons, climb to ridges delineated by drystone walling. As the valley's shoulders converge, there is barely elbow room for the lines of communication to forge their way towards the summit. The most potent image of this conflict is at GAUXHOLME, where the railway works a 'one-two' with the canal, one of its crossings being a Gothically inspired, cast iron bridge with crenellated abutments as photogenic from the neighbouring hillside, as anything anywhere on the inland waterway system. By the top of the Gauxholme Three a handsome warehouse with arched loading bay stands alongside the canal.

Locks with lovely names like Nip Square and Winterbutlee lift the Rochdale out of a landscape of mills into a landscape of sheep and isolated hill farms. The short intervening pounds have a predilection for loosening their stays and spilling over into fleshy, reedy margins. Presumably this was an aid to water supply, along with the canal company's eight reservoirs which gleam like aluminium up on the moorland tops. Given the notorious inclination to rain that this part of the world 'enjoys', it is hard to conceive that water supply was ever a problem. But, it was, and in their heyday the reservoirs supplied up to four million gallons a day to the canal through a network of feeder channels. All the reservoirs were sold to the Rochdale and Oldham corporations in 1923, on the understanding that sufficient water levels would be maintained on the canal. Not that such supplies were needed much longer in the cause of navigation, for the last through barge crossed the summit in the Thirties.

The summit is 601 feet above sea level. The adjoining railway, engineered by George Stephenson only forty years after completion of the canal, tunnels under the highest point of the gorge in order to reduce the steepness of its approach gradients. Diesels hoot hauntingly as they enter the tunnel's decorated portals, contributing to the sense of isolation. The old Todmorden Turnpike road passes a toll house at Warland where West Yorkshire gives way, as gracefully as possible in the circumstances, to Greater Manchester. Nearby the Bird i' th' Hand (Tel: 01706 378145) offers food and a congenial atmosphere - just the thing to raise moral in lock-weary mountaineers.

*J*UST as a stranger can find it difficult to differentiate between the accents and dialects of Lancashire and Yorkshire, so too is it hard to draw a distinction between the landscapes. Closer scrutiny suggested a tendency to austerity at the western end of the summit level, a greater inclination to use brick which lacks the warmth and harmony of local stone. But perhaps it was simply the rain, descending like nine inch galvanised nails, which coloured our perceptions as we came down from the six hundred feet contour on our initial research trip, senses still reeling from the high octane entertainment provided by this spectacular canal.

With the little River Roch in tow, the Rochdale Canal gets quickly 'stuck in', as a series of locks carry it down past the old Rock Nook cotton mills. Did you notice how the Roch is taken over the railway by the western portal of Summit Tunnel in an iron trough?

We keep referring to this as 'Lancashire', but since the crass local government reorganisations of the mid Seventies, no part of the Rochdale Canal lies in Lancashire at all! Here, heaven help us, we're in Greater Manchesterland. The canal does its best to rise above the imperfections of political boundaries, although it is noticeable that the locks are less well-appointed on this side, though continued difficulties with water supplies often render the summit unnavigable.

By Benthouse Lock a slender, angled dock complete with stump of crane hints at former commerce. Although shown on the 1911, 6in OS map, no corresponding works caught our eye. Perhaps there was some intercourse with Stephenson's new fangled railway, or with the quarry at nearby Windy Bank. Several mills have disappeared. Durn Mill dealt, unusually for Lancashire, in woollens.

The outskirts of Littleborough turn a somewhat blank face as the canal skirts its eastern periphery. For six years since the Rochdale's re-opening in 1996, Littleborough marked the somewhat low-key terminus of navigation. In 2002, however, the canal was restored to navigable status southwards from here over the remaining 17 miles and 35 locks of its original route to Manchester, thus creating a new South Pennine Ring which, theoretically at least, should encourage boating levels to a new high in the context of northern waters. The remaining miles to Manchester feature in the 7th edition of our Cheshire Ring guide. Join us there!

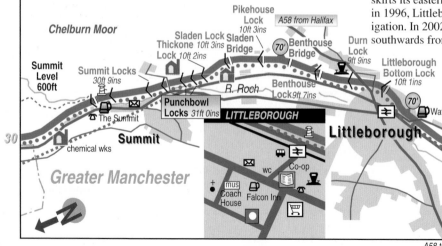

Chelburn Moor

Pikehouse Lock 10ft 3ins

A58 from Halifax

Sladen Lock 10ft 3ins Sladen Bridge
Thickone Lock 10ft 2ins

Benthouse Bridge 70'

Durn Lock 9ft 9ins

Littleborough Bottom Lock 10ft 1ins

Summit Level 600ft

Summit Locks 30ft 9ins

Punchbowl Locks 31ft 0ins

R. Roch

Benthouse Lock 9ft 7ins

The Summit

chemical wks

LITTLEBOROUGH

Summit

Littleborough

70'

Waterside Inn

Greater Manchester

Co-op

wc

mus

Coach House   Falcon Inn

A58 to Rochdale (2mls)   To Rochdale 2miles

The
HUDDERSFIELD
Canal

WE were not expecting much of the Huddersfield Broad, consequently we enjoyed it enormously. Firstly, though, we had to hit on its shy, low-profile egress from the Calder & Hebble in the neighbourhood of Cooper Bridge. Bottomley's mill chimney (aka Holme Spinning Co) serves as a useful landmark, but extreme caution is required from boaters if they are to avoid being drawn towards a sizeable weir on the Calder, immediately upstream of which, on the right hand side, lies the entrance lock to the Huddersfield Broad, beneath a slender towpath bridge bearing a triangular bridge plate numbered 'H5'.

LOCK No.1 is prettily overlooked by the keeper's cottage, invariably guarded by a large, but seemingly docile (well, from a distance, anyway) Dobermann. An interpretation board offers a few salient facts regarding the "Broad's" history and commercial use. Also known as Sir John Ramsden's Canal (after a local landowner instrumental in its promotion) the canal sets off from Cooper Bridge on a surprisingly rural four mile journey into the heart of Huddersfield.

Passing under the main Trans-Pennine railway line, and negotiating Lock No.2, the canal slips through a water treatment works and past Mamas & Papas factory. The pound between locks 3 and 4 is framed by abandoned railway viaducts and overlooked by a large dyeworks which used to get its sulphur from Widnes by barge via the Rochdale Canal. The first viaduct, of fifteen blue brick arches, is a relic of the Midland Railway's ill-timed expansionism prior to the First World War. It belonged to the same misplaced optimism as the abandoned line between Calder Grove and Dewsbury which was to have speeded Anglo-Scottish traffic through the West Riding. The second viaduct, embellished with yellow brick eyebrows above its blue arches, carried the London & North Western Railway's 'Kirkburton Dick' push & pull locals across the Colne Valley until they steamed into oblivion back in 1930. When the viaduct was being built, one of its arches fell into the canal.

A former corn mill stands alongside the A62 road bridge at DEIGHTON. A most attractive pound ensues, with a swarthily wooded railway embankment on one side and an array of sports fields on the other. A notice board advises passers-by to keep an eye out for stray javelins. Locks materialise at frequent

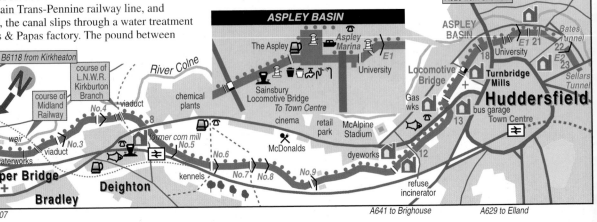

intervals as the canal traverses a quasi rural landscape interspersed with pockets of woodland and a continuing abundance of work's playing fields. Across the A62 the football teams get paid for playing at Huddersfield Town's futuristic Alfred McAlpine stadium. Herbert Chapman, manager here in the Twenties when 'Town' won the league championship three times in a row, would have approved. The high chimney of the municipal incinerator soars above the canal in a manner reminiscent of a similar installation on the Wolverhampton 'Twenty-One'.

Less than a mile to go now, and the old industries, which once took so much advantage of canal transport, close in about the cut, creating shadowy canyons of cargo-carrying memories. Dog-legging under Leeds Road and passing a gasworks, Waterloo Mills and a waterside church, the Huddersfield Broad reaches its most famous installation, the Locomotive (or Turnbridge) Bridge, a Heath Robinsonish contraption, 'designed' - if that is not too functional a verb in this circumstance - to lift for the passage of boats. A sanitary station key is required to unlock the structure, but operation is by hand with a winch.

Thereafter the canal approaches ASPLEY BASIN somewhat anti-climactically. Much of the old ambience has been swept away with the erection of a huge Sainsbury supermarket on one side and a modern pub on the other. At least their presence, and that of a small boatyard, provides a sense of security for mooring up to explore the entertaining town of Huddersfield. Historically, the Broad Canal continued for a quarter of a mile, making a connection with the River Colne. Nowadays this short stretch of canal is dominated by the buildings of Huddersfield University.

The Huddersfield Narrow Canal begins its twenty mile journey across the Pennines at Lock E1 - E being for 'east'. The lock is overlooked by mills refurbished for use by the university. Considerable engineering work was required to restore this section of the canal. Industrial premises had been built over the bed of the canal and in order to by-pass these obstructions it was necessary to lower the canal. Lock 2 was moved west and to reach it the canal passes through a newly built tunnel under the works of Bates & Co Yarn Spinners. The same 'cut & fill' technique was adopted to pass beneath Sellars works to reach a new Lock E3. There is no towpath through these new 'tunnels'.

Lock 3, Huddersfield Broad

Lock 9, Huddersfield Broad

THE Huddersfield Narrow Canal's invigorating traverse of England's Pennine backbone constitutes one of the inland waterways' greatest experiences. Happily, after over a half a century of abandonment, this magnificent canal can be navigated again and enjoyed by a new era of pleasure boaters.

Enjoyed? Well yes, if the thought of operating over seventy locks in less than twenty miles doesn't deter you! Not that it should, for on this wonderful canal physical endeavour is index-linked to pleasure and sense of achievement in equal measure.

Not an easy canal to negotiate, and not an easy canal to build. It was seventeen years in the building; five on the route of the canal, twelve on the great tunnel under Standedge, of which more on Map 34. Furthermore, as observed by Ronald Russell in his classic *Lost Canals & Waterways of Britain,* it was built 'on the cheap', a narrowbeam canal surrounded by widebeam waterways who were better positioned to fight a losing battle with the railways when they came.

Bear all this in mind as you make your way through the Colne Valley. Few canals keep such intimate company with rivers they are topographically attuned to. The Colne is always within earshot if not in view: creaming over weirs, sighing

sullenly through man-made channels. It already worked for a living long before the canal came; powering, flushing and cooling for industry.

At Paddock canal, railway and river form a photogenic whole which finds a strange mirror image at Saddleworth - see Map 36. Here the canal is carried over the Colne on a masonry aqueduct which incorporates Lock E5. Towering above this unusual arrangement is Sir John Hawkshaw's imposing railway viaduct of 1850, an attractively curvaceous mix of masonry arches and flat latticed ironwork spans. The Colne is bridged again in the vicinity of Golcar, as the canal zig-zags through a wooded locality which engenders a typical sense of isolation in an otherwise heavily urbanised valley.

Massive textile mills punctuate the valley, none more magnificent than Titanic Mills between locks 16 and 17; defenestrated but defiant, requiring only money and imagination - in equally massive amounts - to be revived.

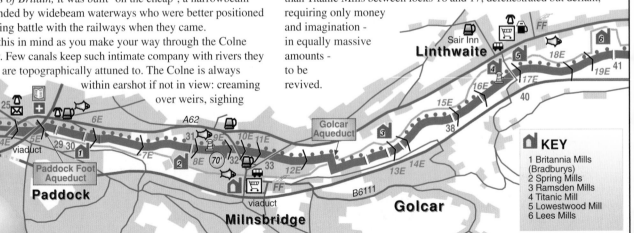

KEY
1 Britannia Mills (Bradburys)
2 Spring Mills
3 Ramsden Mills
4 Titanic Mill
5 Lowestwood Mill
6 Lees Mills

WUTHERING HEIGHTS springs to mind as you negotiate the charismatic scenery of the upper Colne Valley. Climbing to (and descending from) the highest navigable pound (645ft above sea level) on the British canal system, the Huddersfield Narrow Canal is characterised by the austerity of the valley's high ridges and rough pastures, its mill villages and its stone domestic dwellings, doggedly clinging to the earth with gritted teeth in the face of funnelled gales.

Remarkably transformed by restoration, the canal strides through Slaithwaite with the misplaced nonchalance of a package tourist. The return of the canal here succinctly demonstrates the enormous benefits to be had from regenerating canals in an urban environment. Life has returned to the main thoroughfare, with its shops along the north bank of the canal and the massive premises of the grandiloquently named Globe Worsted Company casting its shadow from the south.

Between Slaithwaite and Marsden the canal is at its most bucolic. Whether on foot or afloat, make sure you soak up this landscape; drink it all in, from the ponies in the waterside pastures to the stark, horizon-bounding ridges.

Cellars Clough Mill and the neighbouring Sandhill cottages form an attractive group beside Sparth Reservoir, one of ten built by the canal company to ensure adequate water supplies on such a heavily locked route. The canal actually climbs a total of 438 feet on its eastern side, from which you will extrapolate that the locks average around ten and half feet per chamber. By the time the westbound traveller reaches Marsden they come thick and fast. Standedge towers above you, brooking no argument, as if you're being pursued and have reached a cul de sac. Some dead end! Standedge's western portal looks

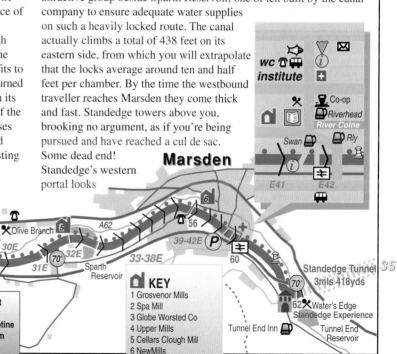

KEY
1 Grosvenor Mills
2 Spa Mill
3 Globe Worsted Co
4 Upper Mills
5 Cellars Clough Mill
6 NewMills

Lock 24E at Slaithwaite has a guillotine style bottom gate.

Standedge Tunnel 3mls 418yds

Mill with terraces, Slaithwaite

like a mousehole in a wainscot. The closer to it you come, the more you have to crane your neck to see the moorland high above you, its tawny skin scarred by wart-like growths of spoil long ago left over from the excavation of the tunnels.

Tunnels plural? Yes, there are *four* of them: the canal tunnel of 1811; the original single bore railway tunnel of 1849; an 1871 duplicate; and a double track railway bore of 1894. The canal tunnel lies below and between the railway tunnels. It features (ultimate accolade!) in the *Guinness Book of Records* as the longest (3 miles, 418 yards), deepest (being a maximum of 638 feet beneath the highest point of the moor) and highest (the summit pound is 645 feet above sea level) in the country. Its construction, given the lack of sophisticated equipment available, is simply astonishing. Travel through it in awe of the boldness of its undertaking, but try also, if you can, to journey over the top (see buses under Marsden in the Gazetteer) and gain a different perspective on the achievement. Sadly the route of Boat Lane, along which horses were led over the top in time honoured canal fashion, has been partially obliterated by subsequent road building programmes, but even a ten minute drive along the A62 will illustrate the tunnel-builders bravery and vision.

The interior of Standedge Tunnel is only intermittently lined. At intervals it widens into limestone caverns of great natural beauty. Four passing places were also provided towards the middle of the tunnel. From time to time you come upon linking passages up to the railway tunnels. These 'adits' were used by the railway builders to extract spoil by boat. In the days of steam dense clouds of railway engine smoke would billow down into the canal tunnel, emerging, in the fullness of time from the Marsden or Diggle portals as though the tunnel were the lair of fiery dragons.

Working boats were 'legged' through Standedge, three and a half hours being the average time to complete a passage. In 1824 a steam tug was tried, but only lasted nine years before the leggers took over again. In any case trade through the tunnel was never exactly brisk, and in the second half of the 19th century the railway quickly attracted the bulk of trade. The last recorded passage of a cargo-carrying boat through the tunnel occurred in 1921. Official abandonment came in 1944, but four years later a party of IWA luminaries navigated the whole of the Huddersfield Narrow in a wooden cruiser called *Ailsa Craig* and both Robert Aickman and Tom Rolt have described that illustrious journey through Standedge Tunnel in their respective autobiographies *The River Runs Uphill* and *Landscape With Canals*. They were so sooty when they reached Marsden, that they had no alternative but to catch a train down into Huddersfield and have a bath at the George Hotel. Aickman wrote that he actually needed *three* baths, one after the other.

Mill chimney reflected, Sparth

STANDEDGE and Saddleworth Moor, unequivocal Pennine landscapes, separated now by the spurious county boundary between West Yorkshire and Greater Manchester, but previously all embraced by Yorkshire's old West Riding. Regular readers will know of (and probably sympathise with) our dislike of the 1974 boundary changes, but, on this rare occasion, there is something apposite about the current frontier, and it seems somehow apt that the metaphorical customs check between the eastern and western sides of the Pennines should, for boaters at least, occur underground; if only it was still the old Lancashire which met you with daylight at the western portal of Standedge Tunnel!

If the tunnel's eastern portal at Marsden resembles a mousehole, here at diggle it has the look of a lock-up garage, and there is barely any sense of high ground beyond. The explanation is that this is not the original western entrance to Standedge, in 1894 the tunnel was lengthend by 220 yards to accommodate the new double track railway tunnel. Prior to that the canal essayed a curving course to the east, entering the hillside in the neighbourhood of the Diggle Hotel.

Thirty-two locks, suffixed on this side of Standedge by the letter W (for West), carry the Huddersfield Narrow Canal down through the Tame Valley to Ashton-under-Lyne. And barely have you emerged from the tunnel before being confronted with the first one. See how they differ from the rest of the canal's locks, being single-gated at each end and featuring curiously angled paddle gear. They are couched in a typically robust Pennine landscape between the railway and Diggle Brook; heather spills over the moss-grown dry-stone wall which borders the towpath. Away to the east, on a ridge of hills known colloquially as the 'pots and pans' an obelisk featured in a number of Lowry's paintings, commemorates the local dead of the Great War. Down in the valley two big works rear their confident heads. Warth Mill was built by the Co-operative Wholesale Society in 1911. In its time it wove both wool and cotton, but now houses various light industries, including a furniture maker. The other, architecturally imposing premises, now occupied by Shaw's pallet factory, was Dobcross Iron Works, concerned with the manufacture of textile looms.

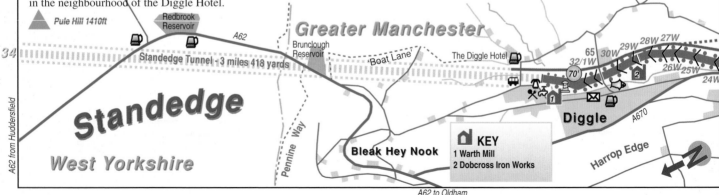

Pule Hill 1410ft · Redbrook Reservoir · A62 · Brunclough Reservoir · Greater Manchester · 'Boat Lane' · The Diggle Hotel · 34 · Standedge Tunnel · 3 miles 418 yards · 65 · 30W · 29W 28W 27W · 32/1W · 26W 25W · 70' · 24W · Standedge · 2 · Diggle · A670 · A62 from Huddersfield · Pennine Way · Bleak Hey Nook · West Yorkshire · **KEY** / 1 Warth Mill / 2 Dobcross Iron Works · Harrop Edge

River Tame and Huddersfield Canal at Uppermill

COMING down from Diggle, the canal encounters a milder Tame Valley, though one given backbone and character by 19th century industrialisation. You fall into a rhythm of lock-working. So much so, that when there's a noticeably longer interval, as occurs between locks 19 and 20, a discomforting sense of withdrawal hovers and your hand strays involuntarily towards your windlass like a production line worker faced with an unexpectedly empty conveyor belt.

Little communities whose economy was once firmly based on textiles add interest to the canal's progress. Some of them, like Uppermill and Dobcross, have reinvented themselves for use in the twenty-first century world of the service and leisure industries; others, notably Mossley, eke out a post-industrial existence still centred on the local mill, the terraced street and the corner house. Entrenched Northern values manifest themselves at Greenfield where that peculiarly Pennine sport, Rugby League, flourishes at a neat little stadium alongside the canal.

The transhipment warehouse at DOBCROSS remains one of the canal's most historic features. Its location marks the terminus of the canal between 1799 and 1811 while the small matter of Standedge was being considered. Luckily the simple but effective structure has survived years of neglect and now proudly overlooks a waterpoint, Elsan disposal provision and visitor moorings picturesquely sited alongside a converted mill.

Nearby stands one of the Huddersfield Narrow's most visually satisfying locations where Saddleworth's curving and imposing railway viaduct straddles the canal at Lock 23W, the latter built into an aqueduct over the River Tame in a similar manner to Lock 4E on the outskirts of Huddersfield.

Another pretty setting is to be found at Lock 19W where the Tame has been dammed to form a reservoir feeding the handsome Royal George Mills, under redevelopment when we last passed. There's a rural interlude here as well, whilst nearby the canal's largest aqueduct carries it across the river in idyllic surroundings of pastureland backed by moorland ridges.

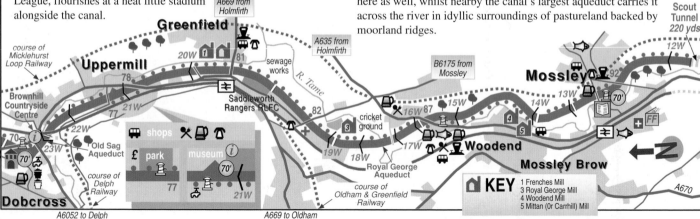

KEY
1 Frenches Mill
3 Royal George Mill
4 Woodend Mill
5 Mittan (0r Carrhill) Mill

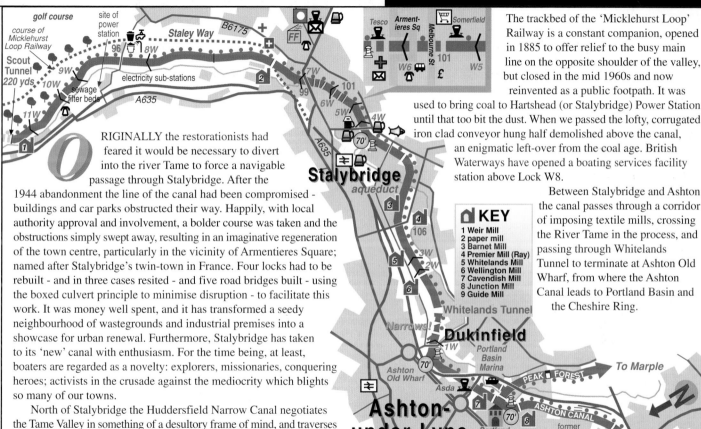

The trackbed of the 'Micklehurst Loop' Railway is a constant companion, opened in 1885 to offer relief to the busy main line on the opposite shoulder of the valley, but closed in the mid 1960s and now reinvented as a public footpath. It was used to bring coal to Hartshead (or Stalybridge) Power Station until that too bit the dust. When we passed the lofty, corrugated iron clad conveyor hung half demolished above the canal, an enigmatic left-over from the coal age. British Waterways have opened a boating services facility station above Lock W8.

Between Stalybridge and Ashton the canal passes through a corridor of imposing textile mills, crossing the River Tame in the process, and passing through Whitelands Tunnel to terminate at Ashton Old Wharf, from where the Ashton Canal leads to Portland Basin and the Cheshire Ring.

RIGINALLY the restorationists had feared it would be necessary to divert into the river Tame to force a navigable passage through Stalybridge. After the 1944 abandonment the line of the canal had been compromised - buildings and car parks obstructed their way. Happily, with local authority approval and involvement, a bolder course was taken and the obstructions simply swept away, resulting in an imaginative regeneration of the town centre, particularly in the vicinity of Armentieres Square; named after Stalybridge's twin-town in France. Four locks had to be rebuilt - and in three cases resited - and five road bridges built - using the boxed culvert principle to minimise disruption - to facilitate this work. It was money well spent, and it has transformed a seedy neighbourhood of wastegrounds and industrial premises into a showcase for urban renewal. Furthermore, Stalybridge has taken to its 'new' canal with enthusiasm. For the time being, at least, boaters are regarded as a novelty: explorers, missionaries, conquering heroes; activists in the crusade against the mediocrity which blights so many of our towns.

North of Stalybridge the Huddersfield Narrow Canal negotiates the Tame Valley in something of a desultory frame of mind, and traverses a messy region of electricity sub-stations and power station ruins.

KEY
1 Weir Mill
2 paper mill
3 Barnet Mill
4 Premier Mill (Ray)
5 Whitelands Mill
6 Wellington Mill
7 Cavendish Mill
8 Junction Mill
9 Guide Mill

*Figures refer to Huddersfield Canal (Scout tunnel to Ashton Old Wharf)

A635 to Manchester   Ashton Canal to Manchester

ADLINGTON
Map 2

Adlington's usefulness to boaters is multiplied by the provision of designated visitor moorings alongside the recreation ground south of bridge 69. The village is also the most practical canalside base camp for the ascent of Rivington Pike a couple of country miles to the east.

WHITE BEAR MARINA CAFE - Boaters breakfasts, burgers etc. Open Tue-Sat, 9am-4pm. Tel: 01257 481054.

GIUSEPPE'S - Tel: 01257 475275. Italian restaurant.

There are also two Indian restaurants and three pubs to choose from. Perhaps best appointed pub is the WHITE BEAR - again on the main road - which usefully offers accommodation (01257 482357).

Co-op store at crossroads 200 yards from bridge 69. Also nearby are a chemist, newsagent, post office and Bank of Scotland. Laundry at marina. Don't forget to call in at FREDERICKS ice cream dairy between bridges 72A and 73. Tel: 01257 263154.

TRAINS: from station half mile east of bridge 69, hourly, daily to/from Manchester, Preston and Blackpool. Tel: 08457 484950. BUSES: local services along A6 corridor. Tel: 01257-241693.

RIVINGTON COUNTRY PARK: 2 miles east of Adlington. Reservoirs, signposted walks, gardens and breathtaking views.

ASHTON-UNDER-LYNE
Map 37

Once all these satellites in Manchester's solar system must have seemed more self sufficiently autonomous, now their economies rely on those too poor or immobile to visit 'big brother' to go about their business. Yet an old pride lingers in the weather-beaten faces of the more elderly locals and, met half way, their town more than repays a visit from passing canallers. Failing that, you could try a faith-healing session in the Town Hall, Mondays 11am to 3pm. Incidentally, this was the birthplace, in 1892, of the travel writer H.V. Morton.

The Market Hall is breathtaking, and it is quite possible to lose your womenfolk in it for hours on end while you attend to more serious matters, like a meat pie from S. Williams & Sons.

WENDY'S MEMORY LANE - Stamford Street. Characterful tea room knee-deep in memorabilia. Tel: 0161 330 2771.

TOURIST INFORMATION - Market Street. Tel: 0161 343 4343.

TRAINS - frequent services to/from Manchester Victoria, Stalybridge and Huddersfield. Tel: 08457 484950.

BUSES - Tel: 0161 228 7811. Useful links throughout the Tame Valley.

BARNOLDSWICK
Map 10

'Barlick', as the locals call it, looks less than inviting from the canal, but its centre, 10 minutes walk from bridges 153 or 154A, is very pleasant indeed, being gathered about the Town Square.

ANCHOR INN (Salterforth - bridge 151): cheerful stone pub pre-dating canal with stalactites in the cellar. Bar meals; families welcome. Tel: 01282 813186. Numerous other pubs, cafes and fish & chips in 'Barlick'.

Post office and garage with shop by bridge 154A, otherwise head for the centre where there's a good Co-op supermarket and a mouthwatering array of baker and butcher shops. Branches of HSBC, Lloyds TSB, Barclays & Yorkshire banks.

BUSES: Pennine services link with Skipton & Colne. Tel: 01756 795515.

TOURIST INFORMATION: Fernlea Ave. Tel: 01282 666708.

BANCROFT MILL: preserved compound stationary steam engine. Regular steaming afternoons. Tel: 01282 813751.

BARROWFORD
Map 9

Attractively strung-out along the banks of Pendle Water, Barrowford lies a worthwhile quarter of an hour's walk along a pavemented road to the west of Bridge 143A.

HERITAGE CENTRE Garden Tea Room (below) for coffees, light lunches and teas.

Local shops cater for most requirements. Bannisters Bakery is especially good.

PENDLE HERITAGE CENTRE: Park Hill. Tel: 01282 661702. Open daily 10am-5.00pm. Fascinating and atmospheric interpretive centre for Pendle past and present. Shop, tea rooms, garden and woodland walk.

BINGLEY
Map 16

The A650's seamless traffic does Bingley few favours, and it remains to be seen whether the long awaited Airedale road will provide any balm. But away from the busy main street, Bingley has its quiet places: a pleasant riverside park, an interesting and substantial parish church, and an old Butter Cross thought to date from 1212 when King John first granted a market charter.

THE FISHERMANS - canalside bridge 205. Popular with boaters, walkers and, yes, fishermen, alike. Bass beers and bar meals. Tel: 01274 564238.

VECCHIO MULINO - Park Road. Tel: 01274 770533. Sardinian restaurant and sandwich bar adjacent to the canal at bridge 202.

Market on Weds & Fris. Branches of most banks. SAFEWAY supermarket adjacent to canal. DAMART factory shop on Park Road.

TRAINS: frequent Metro local services linking Bingley with Skipton, Saltaire, Shipley, Bradford & Leeds. V. useful for towpath walkers.

BLACKBURN
Map 5

The chief of East Lancashire's old textile towns doesn't exactly inspire confidence as a place to drop anchor (let alone eat and drink with any degree of sophistication) but it's a vibrant city and by the time you've retraced your steps to the canal, you may find your preconceptions being changed.

Shopping is one of Blackburn's strong points (though, alas, Sargeson & Mullineaux's corset shop, the elaborately fortified contents of whose window invariably caught one's eye when wandering down from Eanam Wharf, has become a victim of redevelopment) from the fine MARKET HALL to TOMMY BALL'S shoe superstore. There are Asda, Morrisons and Tesco supermarkets all within supermarket trolley submerging distance of the canal.

TRAINS - frequent connections with major centres throughout the region. Handy services along the L&L Corridor via Rishton, Church, Hapton, Rose Grove, Burnley, Brierfield and Nelson to Colne. Tel: 08457 484950.

BUSES - direct link with Chorley, otherwise not available by train. Ribble service 123/4, hourly, daily. Tel: 01772 254754.

TOURIST INFORMATION - Northgate. Tel: 01254 53277. Major visitor attractions include WAVES, an indoor pool with wave simulation and flume; the ARENA ice rink; the ART GALLERY and LEWIS TEXTILE MUSEUM; and the late nineteenth century CATHEDRAL.

BRIERFIELD
Map 8

Useful stop between Burnley and Nelson. Good range of shops, banks and fast food outlets up on the A682. Interesting retail development at PENDLE VILLAGE MILL by Bridge 139.

BRIGHOUSE
Map 26

Best known for its brass band, Brighouse is an engaging little town with a network of largely traffic-free streets made up of shot-blasted clean Victorian stone buildings. Not a lot of people know that Wagner's grand-daughters went to school here.

LA ROMANTICA - Mill Street. Cosy and well established Italian restaurant. Tel: 01484 400114.

PREGO - more Italian cuisine in canalside appendix of Waterfront Lodge offering accommodation. Tel: 01484 715566.

THE BARGE - Mill Lane. Friendly local adjacent canal basin displaying some interesting archive views of the C&H. Tel: 01484 401947.

CZERWIK'S wine & cheese shop (Tel: 01484 720912) on Commercial St continues to be the best reason for coming to Brighouse and there are good butchers and bakers in the town as well. SAINSBURY'S canalside supermarket provides for most other needs and there are NatWest, Barclays and HSBC banks.

TRAINS - re-opened station offering links to Huddersfield and Halifax. Tel: 08457 484950.

BUSES - to most West Riding destinations. Tel: 01422 364467.

BURNLEY
Map 8

Burnley's backdrop of mills and chimneys looks much as it might have done three-quarters of a century ago. Closer inspection, though, exposes the town's post industrial shortcomings: tailbacks on the inner ring-road, litter wafting through the precinct; a hollow, underfed emptiness behind the textile mill windows. But we like Burnley: its imposing municipal buildings, the Ashfield Road viaduct (railway equivalent of the canal embankment spanning the valley of the Brun) and the population's determination to 'get on with life' despite being just a mile or two too far down the M65 to ever fully experience the miracle of industrial regeneration.

BELFIELD'S - prize winning fish & chips by Finsley Gate Wharf.

THE INN ON THE WHARF - canalside Bridge 130B. Tel: 01282 459951. Warehouse conversion open all day. Families welcome.

continued overleaf:

continued from previous page:

🝤 Modern precinct and traffic-free street shopping as befits the "fourth largest centre in Lancashire". Fine MARKET HALL (Mon-Sat ex Tue) plus open air stalls on Mon, Thur & Sat.

🚌 TRAINS: services from Central & Barracks stations to/from Colne & Blackburn. Services from Manchester Road to/from Yorkshire. Tel: 08457 484950. BUSES - Tel: 0870 6082608.

ⓘ TOURIST INFORMATION - Manchester Road. Tel: 01282 664421. WEAVERS TRIANGLE VISITOR CENTRE - Manchester Road (bridge 130B). Open Easter-Sep, Mon-Wed, Sat & Sun afternoons. Tel: 01282 452403.

CALDER GROVE   Map 24

🍺 THE NAVIGATION - canalside below Broad Cut Top Lock. Splendid stone-built inn separated from water's edge by large garden with picnic tables and childrens play area. Inside, it's divided into two distinct zones: a quiet and cosy lounge hung with archive photographs of the Calder & Hebble; and a family bar complete with 'ball play' area. The beer comes from the Barge & Barrel Brewery at Elland (our pints of Nettlethrasher went down admirably on a hot afternoon), whilst amongst a wide menu of bar meals lurks the locally made Hector Ellis pork pie, best taken with mushy peas. Tel: 01924 274361.

🝤 Small general store, newsagents and post office on main road five minutes walk uphill.

CASTLEFORD   Map 23

This famous Rugby League town lies a bleak, but interesting quarter of an hour's walk across the Aire from the Visitor Moorings in Bulholme Cut, though there are modest shopping facilities on Lock Lane. Henry Moore, the sculptor, was born in Castleford, but its prosperity has been derived from making glass and chemicals. On your way into town, look out for Allinson's flour mill. In common with their famous stoneground bread, Castleford is a "town with nowt taken out!"

🍺 BOAT INN - waterside at Allerton Bywater. Tel: 01977 552216. Idyllic waterside pub brewing its own ales. Food always available and families welcome. Sadly no official mooring jetty, but well worth improvising for.

🝤 Surprisingly substantial shopping centre called Carlton Lanes in the heart of town, but it's a long way back over Castleford Bridge with packages unless you can be bothered to unravel the local bus timetable.

CHORLEY   Map 3

Cakes are Chorley's claim to fame, a sticky, fruity pastry of the Eccles ilk much favoured locally, but difficult to find elsewhere. And sadly, the centre of town is perhaps just too far from the canal for the average boater to take much notice of it, though, there are points of interest, such as Tuesday's "Flat Iron" market and Astley Hall, a 16th century mansion owned by the local authority, which demand further investigation.

🍺 THE RAILWAY - canalside bridge 78A. All day pub offering wide menu. Tel: 01257 279410.

ⓘ BOTANY BAY - Almost indefinable, this converted mill houses an array of antiques and craft businesses, restaurants and memorabilia with accompanying children's play centre called Puddletown Pirates. Bizarre or inspired - we'll let you judge. Tel: 01257 261220. Small entrance fee, open daily 10am-6pm

COLNE   Map 9

Hilltop town, two miles east of Barrowford Locks, notable for its "British in India" museum (01282 870215) devoted to the great days of the Raj. Colne was the home of Wallace Hartley, conductor of the "Titanic's" heroic band who played "Nearer My God to Thee" as the liner went down. But Colne's main use to user's of this guide is likely to be perceived as that of a staging-post with useful transport facilities for towpath walkers.

🚌 TRAINS - terminus of branch from Burnley Central, daily service running through to Blackpool. Tel: 08457 484950 . BUSES - connections with Skipton via Barnoldswick. Tel: 0870 608 2 608 or 01756 795515.

DEWSBURY
Map 25

Typical West Riding woollen town, best known these days for the large retail market (where the emphasis is still very much on textiles) held on Wednesdays and Saturdays. The town centre lies across the Calder, about twenty minutes trudge from Savile Town Basin.

LEGGERS - Town Wharf. Tel: 01924 502846. Loft conversion of boat horse stables overlooking terminus basin. Food and range of beers. Also adjoining bistro and coffee shop.

WEST RIDING REFRESHMENT ROOMS - atmospheric railway station bar. Food and range of beers. Tel: 01924 459193.

DIGGLE
Map 35

There seems something comic, faintly music hall, about Diggle, or at least its name; though if you've just spent three subterranean hours in Standedge Tunnel you may well be hysterical enough already. The truth, as always, is more prosaic, and this little textile village huddles for protection in the folds of moorland which sweep up to the darkest part of the Pennines.

DIGGLE HOTEL - Station Houses, 2 mins walk from Diggle portal. Tel: 01457 872741. Sombre stone facade belies a warm welcome in this blissfully noise-free pub. Food, accommodation and Timothy Taylor's 'Landlord'.

DIGGLE NOOK BISTRO - Sam Road (adjacent tunnel portal). Tel: 01457 810044.

PRINGLES - quaint fish & chip cabin featuring Hollands Pies from Baxendale. Also worth trying: THE HANGING GATE, village centre pub with nice tiled entrance.

A post office (manned by a lovely lady with an infectious laugh) forms the sum total of Diggle's shopping facilities, the imposing Co-operative premises on Sam Road having been converted into office accommodation.

BUSES - No.184 operates hourly Mon to Sat all the way from Diggle's moorland fringed terminus to the fleshpots of Manchester Piccadilly Gardens by way of Oldham - more a life-enhancing experience than a mere bus ride. Tel: 0161 228 7811. On Sundays there's a useful link for towpath walkers with Marsden and Huddersfield.

DOBCROSS
Map 36

Another of Saddleworth's constituent villages. Picturesque hilltop location which was effectively used in the 1980 movie *Yanks*.

THE NAVIGATION - adjacent canal at Wool Road (Lock W24). CAMRA recommended, brass band orientated pub offering food and a variety of beers. Tel: 01457 872418.

SWAN INN - The Square. Blessedly quiet, 18th century hilltop, stone-flagged local dispensing home made meals and Jenning's beer.

BROWNHILL COUNTRYSIDE CENTRE - canalside above Lock W23. Tel: 01457 872598. Information and exhibitions on the Tame Valley's environment.

EAST MARTON
Map 11

Heavenly stopover high up in the Dales with, appropriately enough, a lovely church with a Norman tower, though the interior was much 'improved' by the Victorians. Moor the boat and stretch your legs along the "Pennine Way".

CROSS KEYS - overlooking bridge 161 (though quieter approach from 162). Classic country pub offering a wonderfully varied menu of bar and restaurant food. Tel: 01282 843485.

ABBOT'S HARBOUR - adjacent bridge 162. Delightful cafe/restaurant also dealing in postcards, local books, confectionary etc and offering bed & breakfast. Tel: 01282 843207.

ELLAND
Map 27

Characterful little industrial town on a hill above the Calder. The bridge dates back to the 17th century, though with subsequent lengthenings and widenings. Notable businesses include Dobson's sweet factory .

BARGE & BARREL - lunches and lots of guest beers beside the canal. Tel: 01422 373623.

COLLIERS ARMS - canalside below Elland Lock. The landlord is a boat-owner himself and couldn't have been more helpful to our research crew marooned without running water. Sam Smith's beer and bar meals served in an attractive conservatory overlooking the canal. Childrens room and moorings for patrons. Tel: 01422 372704.

Elland provides good shopping facilities and gravity should aid your package-laden progress back to the boat. Branches of Lloyds TSB, Yorkshire, NatWest and Barclays banks. Dobson's retail sweety shop on Southgate.

FOULRIDGE
Map 9

A deservedly popular overnight stop for boaters, Foulridge marks the westernmost limit of many a hire boat itinerary before industry begins to make an impression. The village itself is indeed an attractive base from which to explore the surrounding countryside, and there are many pleasant walks to be had in the vicinity of the canal's reservoirs. A trip boat operates public services on Sundays and Tuesdays throughout the season, and there is also a day boat for hire. Tel: 01282 844033. *continued overleaf*

continued from previous page:

🫖 The HOLE IN THE WALL (Tel: 01282 863568) celebrates the adventures of 'Buttercup" the amphibious cow, but you might also try the HARE & HOUNDS (Tel: 01282 863070) up on the main road. There is also a Chinese take-away.

🏭 Newsagents & general store, off licence and butcher. CROFT MILL SHOP sells a variety of fabrics. Tel: 01282-869625.

🚌 Pennine Motors link Foulridge with Barnoldswick, Colne and Skipton. Tel: 01756 795515.

GARGRAVE   Map 12

If Skipton is the Leeds & Liverpool Canal's nicest town, Gargrave qualifies as its most pleasant large village. It has set out its stall to cater for visitors ever since the inception of the Pennine Way, and now welcomes discerning canal users, whether they be on foot or afloat, as well. Leaving one of the crew to replenish the water tank, we went in search of ice cream and came upon a village which quickly captivated us with its charming houses.

🫖 ANCHOR INN - canalside bridge 169A. Busy 'Brewers Fayre' family pub with extensive gardens. Accommodation. Tel: 01756 749666.
BOLLYWOOD COTTAGE - village centre. Tel: 01756 749252. Indian restaurant and take-away.
MASON'S ARMS - opposite church. Cosy and welcoming local. Food and families. Tel: 01756 749304.
DALESMAN CAFE - village centre - high starch meals for hungry cyclists and walkers. Tel: 01756 749250.

🏭 Useful range of shops including small supermarket, chemist, newsagent, post office and antiques.

🚌 TRAINS - sparse local service on the scenic line to Lancaster via Giggleswick with connections southwards to Skipton and Leeds. Tel: 08457 484950.
BUSES - Pennine Motors to/from Settle and Skipton plus occasional links with Malham (for the tarn, cove, and Gordale Scar). Tel: 01756 749215.

GREENFIELD   Map 36

Mill village useful for its railway station. Good well-appointed J.W.Lees inn called THE ROYAL GEORGE (Tel: 01457 837851) at junction of B6175 and A635 east of Bridge 82.

HAPTON   Map 7

Reputedly the first village in England to be provided (in 1888) with domestic electricity, courtesy of a local entrepreneur whose family went on to be early manufacturers of cinematic equipment and magnetos for motor cars. Consisting of two pubs, a fish & chip shop, newsagent, general store and post office, Hapton is now a useful point of disembarkation for boaters to stretch their legs in the long, lockless pound between Blackburn and Burnley. With the benefit of bicycles, you could make an excursion to the neighbouring town of Padiham where Gawthorpe Hall is open to the public.

HEBDEN BRIDGE   Map 29

Hebden's economy no longer relies on the manufacture of fustian, a sort of thick, twilled cloth, but on attracting tourists. There are even New Age overtones which make it appear, at times, like a northern version of Totnes. But in its setting, deep within the wooded folds of the Calder gorge, and in its sturdy, honey-coloured stone buildings, it transcends any tendency to quaintness, whilst there are many fascinating nooks and crannies waiting to be discovered by the diligent explorer.

🫖 Burgeoning quantities of eating places bear witness to HB's increasing popularity with visitors. On Market Street three establishments caught our eye: THE SWISS CONNECTION, ORGANIC HOUSE and JAVA LOUNGE.
FOX & GOOSE - on A646 at western end of town. Peaceful real-ale enthusiasts' pub. Tel: 01422 842649.
STUBBING WHARF - canalside above Stubbing Locks. Cosy pub offering food. Tel: 01422 844107.
BARGE BRANWELL - tea & coffee from a converted keel, plus canal crafts.

Natwest, Yorkshire, Barclays and Lloyds TSB banks, small market on Thursdays. Co-op supermarket adjacent to Hebble End, plus heaps of 'quaint' little shops, antiques and second-hand bookshops. Several excellent bakers and butchers.

TRAINS - frequent Calder Valley service connecting with Sowerby Bridge and Todmorden, good for towpath walks. Tel: 08457 484950.
BUSES - Yorkshire Rider services duplicate the rail corridor but also offer panoramic journeys up over t'moors to Burnley and Keighley etc. Tel: 01422 365985.

TOURIST INFORMATION - New Road. Tel: 01422 843831. New expanded premises (catering for Hebden's increasing visitor-count) incorporate several admirable canal interpretive displays and some nice models and reliefs.
CALDER VALLEY CRUISING - The Marina. Tel: 01422 845557. Regular tug trips as well as horse-drawn excursions to Walkleys and 'themed' cruises.

HUDDERSFIELD
Map 32

Hugely enjoyable northern town, justifiably proud of its pole position on the newly restored Huddersfield Narrow Canal. Don't rush through, moor up and explore its dignified streets of Victorian architecture. Northern pride personified!

HEAD OF STEAM - St George's Square. Lively real ale pub occupying part of Huddersfield's magnificent railway station. Good for food as well as atmosphere. Lots of railway memorabilia.Tel: 01484 454533.
TRAIN STATION TAVERN - St George's Square. As above plus jazz and blues. Tel: 01484 511058.
THE BLUE ROOMS - Byram Arcade (Westgate). Open Mon-Sat. Superb wholefood restaurant and coffee house tucked away at the rear of a two storey Victorian arcade. A tendency to become crowded at lunchtime, so get there as early as you can. Tel: 01484 512373.

Excellent shopping centre in streets still laid out in a human, as opposed to car, friendly pattern where the specialist retailers can afford the rents to rub shoulders with the big boys. Memorable pork pies (best eaten warm in Yorkshire style) from Mitchell's butchers shop in Station Street - Tel: 01484 531410.

TRAINS - frequent services to major Pennine centres. Tel: 08457 484950.

TOURIST INFORMATION - Albion Street. Tel: 01484 430808.

KEIGHLEY
Map 15

Unexpectedly substantial town lurking a mile across the Aire from the canal at Stockbridge. Revered in beer drinking circles as the home of Timothy Taylor's prize-winning ales, and amongst railway enthusiasts as the junction for the Worth Valley Railway (Tel: 01535 647777) which will carry you up into Bronteland and the haunts of "The Railway Children". Canalside, STOCKBRIDGE and RIDDLESDEN offer typical suburban facilities: some corner shops, a Co-op 'late shop', a butcher and chemist, one or two pubs, fish & chips and a handy launderette. Thus it's strange to come upon, in such surroundings, the National Trust's EAST RIDDLESDEN HALL, a 17th century manor house and tithe barn surrounded by fishponds. Open Easter to October (though not daily) further details can be had on 01535 607075.

KILDWICK
Map 14

Charming village 'twinned' with Farnhill on the opposite bank of the canal. Good spot to moor overnight. THE WHITE LION (Tel: 01535 632265) is a pleasant pub where families are welcome and food is available lunchtimes and evenings.

LEEDS
Map 19

Having been wooed and won by the riverfront, we were in the mood to like Leeds, and it didn't let us down. If Manchester (as we've said elsewhere) is the great plutocrat of the North, Leeds is its sleek mistress. A class act, endowed with busty public buildings, notably the Town Hall and the Corn Exchange, both designed by local architect, Cuthbert Broderick, in the middle of the nineteenth century when Leeds was bareback riding to prominence on the back of the Industrial Revolution, making household names of Hudswell Clarke, Kitsons, Fowlers and their ilk. Likewise, Leeds reinvented itself during the financial boom at the end of the 1980s, and as a centre of finance (or credit as they deftly call it these days) it claims to rival London. And so wandering in to the centre, we found a city apparently 'pleased as Punch' with itself, wheeling and dealing its way through another buying and selling day; its populace whooping up Briggate and whirling along The Headrow like leaves in an Autumn gale. Their enthusiasm - whatever the cause, however misplaced - was infectious, and we loved every minute of our stay in the headquarters of Tykeland.
continued overleaf:

continued from previous page:

THE ADELPHI - adjacent south end of Leeds Bridge. Wonderfully ornate city bar of Edwardian origin. Lunchtime food on weekdays, Tetley beer pumped, we wondered, direct from the brewery? Tel: 0113 245 6377.

DIMITRI'S - Dock Street. Tel: 0113 246 0339. Stylish Greek taverna and tapas bar - offshoot of the one at Castlefield, Manchester featured in our Cheshire Ring guide.

LA COMIDA - Mill Hill (adjacent rail station). Tel: 0113 244 0500. Lively Spanish/Italian restaurant run by football-mad exile from Barcelona.

POOL COURT AT 42 - riverside by Calls Bridge. Gastronomically, ambiently and financially sophisticated restaurant; perfect antidote to a hard day on the river. Tel: 0113 244 4242. Aperitifs on a balcony over the Aire. Closed on Suns and Sat lunchtime. Less formal adjunct in BRASSERIE 44.

Leeds likes to remind you that it was the birthplace of Marks & Spencer. But they've come a long way since the Penny Bazaar, and this is now one of the great shopping centres of the North, commercially and topographically refined; a far cry from the treadmills of Meadowhall. Look out especially for: GRANARY WHARF, a canalside development of craft shops and the like in the vaults below the railway station; the VICTORIA QUARTER a trio of sophisticated arcades; KIRKGATE MARKET, a typically splendid northern indoor market hall; and the elliptically-shaped and domed CORN EXCHANGE with its specialist outlets and open-plan cafes.

TRAINS - city station is just three minutes walk from Granary Wharf. Tel: 08457 484950. BUSES - Tel: 0113 245 7676.

(i) TOURIST INFORMATION - City Station. Tel: 0113 247 8301.
ARMLEY MILLS - canalside bridge 225. Tel: 0113 263 7861. Open daily (ex Mon). Displays of Leeds's industrial history.

THWAITE MILLS - canalside below Knostrop Fall Lock (Map 20). Tel: 0113 249 6453. Open daily (ex Mon). Restored watermill.

KIRKSTALL ABBEY - 10 minutes walk from bridge 221A (Map 18). Tel: 0113 275 5821. Ruined abbey and museum of domestic history featuring reconstructed Victorian street and shops.

LINTHWAITE
Map 33

Colne Valley 'comma' on A62 chiefly notable for characterful, self-brewing SAIR INN (Tel: 01484 842370), an ultimately steep walk up from Lock 17 past the marvellousTitanic Mill. Very good 'fisheries' as well!

LITTLEBOROUGH
Map 31

A traveller in the days before the canal or railway came to Littleborough, found it "a very desirable retreat when it is found impossible to ascend the mountains, during the continuance of the howling storm." Nothing much has changed, for there is still an inclination to sit tight in Littleborough, waiting for the skies to clear before tackling the summit.

FALCON INN - old coaching inn located on A58. Tel: 01706 378640.

THE WATERSIDE INN - canalside. Food and accommodation. Tel: 01706 376250.

THE SUMMIT - cosy pub adjacent to western end of canal summit. Thwaites beer, bar & restaurant meals. Tel: 01706 378011.

Surprisingly extensive facilities including: Co-op supermarket adjacent to railway station. Nat West, Barclays and Yorkshire banks. Antiquarian bookshop. Launderette on Victoria Street.

TRAINS - half-hourly Calder Valley link with Todmorden and Rochdale;
(hourly with Walsden). Tel: 08457 484950.

(i) COACH HOUSE HERITAGE CENTRE - Tel: 01706 378481. Closed Mondays. Exhibitions of Littleborough's history and tearooms. Also Tourist Information.

MARSDEN
Map 34

Erstwhile home of the poet Simon Armitage, this quintessential Pennine mill village is full of character (or should that be characters?) though it is devastatingly no longer the terminus of Huddersfield trolleybus service No.40 The superb Mechanics Institute is headquarters of the Mikron Theatre Company who've been travelling the canals dispensing entertainment and inspiration in equal dollops for thirty years.

TUNNEL END INN - Home made steak pies plus TT's 'Landlord' and Black Sheep beers; 'real ale, real food, real people'. Tel: 01484 844636.

THE RAILWAY - adjacent lock 42E. Burtonwood beers and a good choice of food. Tel: 01484 841541.

RIVERHEAD BREWERY TAP - Peel Street. Evenings only (except for Sunday) this former grocery shop now serves the owners' own ales bearing an inspired choice of names featuring local reservoirs. Tel: 01484 841270.

SWAN HOTEL - Station Road. Accommodation, lunches and a jukebox- free calm are the strengths of this likeable little local a hop, skip and a jump downhill from the canal. Tel: 01484 844308.

MOZARELLA'S PENNINE TEAROOMS - Peel Street, village centre. The metropolis comes to Marsden - stylish cafe bar! Tel: 01484 845511.

THE OLIVE BRANCH - restaurant and accommodation on A62 a mile east of Marsden most easily accessed from Lock E29. Tel: 01484 844487.

Other pubs, fish & chips and ethnic takeaways in the village centre.

There's something pleasingly 'new age' about Marsden's shops, a quality which dovetails neatly with the more traditional aspects of a Pennine textile community. The Co-op stocks most requisites, but better still, patronise the specialists: bakery, butcher, general stores, greengrocer, wholefood shop, outdoor clothing specialist, toyshop and chemist.

(i) **STANDEDGE VISITOR CENTRE** - canalside near tunnel mouth. Car-parking by station followed by a short walk or ride on water taxi. Imaginative conversion of former canal workshop into interpretive centre for the restored canal. Upgraded 2004. Refreshements and rides into the tunnel. Tel: 01484 844298. *www.standedge.co.uk*

MARSDEN MOOR ESTATE - 5685 acres of spectacular National Trust moorland: public access, guided walks and events. Information office located in former railway goods yard adjacent to Marsden station. Tel: 01484 847016.

MARSDEN INFORMATION CENTRE - local facts and figures. Tel: 01484 845595.

MIKRON THEATRE COMPANY - Marsden is the home of this famous canal travelling theatre group. Tel: 01484 843701 for appearance details etc.

TRAINS - hourly local service providing very useful towpath links along the Colne and Tame valleys. Tel: 08457 484950.

BUSES - frequent services to/from Huddersfield and Oldham. Service 365 will take you 'over the top', a salutary lesson in the early 19th century tunnellers achievement. Tel: 0113 245 7676.

MILNSBRIDGE   *Map 33*

Useful suburban community straddling the Colne and backed by a lofty railway viaduct and imposing mill. Facilities include: pubs, cafes, takeaways; KwikSave, chemist, butcher, post office and newsagent; HSBC, Lloyds TSB and Barclays banks. Incidentally, there's a superbly unspoilt fish & chip shop (Moby Dick's) to be found up on the A62. Frequent buses to/from Huddersfield - Tel: 0113 245 7676.

MIRFIELD   *Map 25*

If you had copies of previous editions you'll know we have a soft spot for Mirfield, disparagingly summed up as "useful" by a more famous waterway guide. We saw beyond this faint praise: discovering that Charlotte Bronte was educated (and later taught) here; falling for the post-woollen beauty of South Brook and Ledgard mills; catching sight of one of Mirfield's own Longstaff double-deckers filling with workers at dawn; and meandering up the asphalt lane to pay homage to the old engine sheds which briefly housed a number of Vincent Raven's puissant B16s. But the six intervening years haven't been totally kind to Mirfield. No longer could we find any corned beef and baked bean pies for sale, one of the mills had been demolished, and there was just the faintest, unsubstantiated evidence that the dead hand of uniformity and globalisation was having an adverse effect on this once so characterful little town.

THE NAVIGATION - canalside Station Road. Homely inn set back from canal bank offering Black Sheep and John Smith's beers and lunches. Families welcome. Tel: 01924 492476.

THE SHIP - Shepley Bridge. 'Hungry Horse' family pub overlooking unnavigable reach of the Calder. Tel: 01924 493364.

CALDER ROAD FISHERIES - mouthwatering fish & chips (not Mon/Tue eves) south of bridge 17 beyond the railway bridge.

C&J's SANDWICH SHOP - to south of Bridge 17. Tel: 01924 490981.

KASHMIR RESTAURANT - Indian eat in or takeaway on the main road. Tel: 01924 498786.

LIDL and **CO-OP** (incorporating Post Office) handily placed by Visitor Moorings close to Bridge 18. Banks include: Barclays, HSBC and Nat West.

TRAINS - frequent connections with Wakefield, Leeds & Huddersfield. Tel: 08457 484950.

MOSSLEY
Map 36

Gritty little textile community encompassing both banks of the Tame and rising to its moorland shoulders in rows of stone built terrace housing. Railway station and useful shops and pubs. We were particulalrly taken with the tiny fish & chip shop uphill to the east of the canal. Our fish was fried - while we waited - in a sixty year old frying range, and the owner sang *Strangers in the Night* to the accompaniment of loudly bubbling fat.

NELSON
Map 9

The story goes that Nelson, formerly known as Marsden, got its new name when the Lancashire & Yorkshire Railway company tired of passengers ending up at Marsden (Yorks) when they really wanted to be in Marsden (Lancs) - see above! But anyway Marsden turned itself into Nelson and never looked back, becoming quite a large cotton town towards the end of the nineteenth century, and quite a large administrative centre, for the Borough of Pendle, towards the end of the twentieth.

No pubs or restaurants leap out to recommend themselves in the neighbourhood, but Nelson's shops are full of character. Try MELLINS the butcher on Pendle Street (opposite the imposing mosque) whose black pudding will melt in your mouth. Across the road SALTERS make their ice cream to a recipe dating back to 1945. In the adjacent Cross Street Market two fishmongers vie for your custom: BRAMWELLS and OGDENS.

TRAINS - local services along the Colne-Burnley line. Tel: 08457 484950.

TOURIST INFORMATION - Town Hall. Tel: 01282 692890.

PENDLE WAVELENGTHS - Leeds Road. Tel: 01282 693287. "Tropical indoor paradise."

RISHTON
Map 6

Large village with a tendency to dourness but offering some useful small shops for passing canallers.

BRIDGE CAFE - hot meals for hungry boaters. THE ROEBUCK - congenial 18th century coaching inn. Tel: 01254 884500.

HSBC & Lloyds TSB banks. Greengrocers and chemist, post office, newsagent and general stores. Gift shop.

ROSE GROVE
Map 7

Burnley suburb with good mooring potential. Facilities include post office, general store, chemist, butcher, two newsagents and two fish & chip shops. Of the latter, BIRDS (overlooking the station) has nostalgic photographs on its walls of the old steam engine depot.

SALTAIRE
Map 16

In the good old days you could get to Saltaire by trolleybus crammed with millworkers. Now it's on the tourist map, and Bradford's trolleybus network - though the last in Britain to lower its poles - ceased operating in 1972. But however you come here now, the journey's still worth the making, for though spruced-up beyond all recognition, and no longer wrapped in a pall of worsted cloth mill chimney smoke, Saltaire is still intact and recognisably as its creator, mid nineteenth century mill owner and philanthropist, Sir Titus Salt, intended it to be. Post-industrial Saltaire was reinvented by another visionary, Jonathan Silver, sadly now deceased, and Salts Mill is his monument just as much as Titus Salt's, illustrating to perfection what can be done with all these crumbling dinosaurs in Wigan, Blackburn, Burnley and Nelson if similar imagination and entrepreneurial skill was employed.

SALTS DINER - Salts Mill. Absolutely brilliant cafe/restaurant on second floor of gigantic mill; wonderful food, wonderful setting. Last orders 4.30pm Tel: 01274 530533.

CAFE IN TO THE OPERA - Salts Mill. Tel: 01274 531163. Open Weds-Suns. Splendid new third floor eating area in operatic setting!

VICTORIA FISHERIES - adjacent bridge 207A. Eat in or take-away fish & chips as only Yorkshire knows how. Tel: 01274 585000.

You'll find difficulty in dragging some of the crew away from SALTS MILL and its wonderful array of retail outlets. More prosaically, there's a SPAR grocery on Titus Street, and a post office and branches of Lloyds TSB and Barclays banks up on the A650.

TRAINS - frequent services along the electrified Aire Valley line to/from Skipton, Leeds and Bradford. Tel: 08457 484950.

1853 GALLERY - Ground Floor, Salts Mill. Exhibits include premier collection of local artist made good, David Hockney.
TOURIST INFORMATION & GIFTS - Victoria Road. Tel: 01274 774993.
SHIPLEY GLEN TRAMWAY - 5 minutes stroll across the Aire from bridge 207A. Victorian cable tramway revelling in its centenary in 1995. Slightly complex operating schedule, but usually open daily throughout the summer plus winter weekends. Tel: 01274 589010. Charming small funfair for children at the top and romantic walks up on t'tops.

SHIPLEY
Map 16

Shipley sulks in the penumbra cast by Saltaire's film star looks; though it is not without a certain sullen charm of its own whilst boaters may find it of some practical use in the otherwise shopless void southwards to Leeds and northwards to Bingley. Useful ALDI supermarket and branch of McDONALDS accessible from footbridge 207D.

SILSDEN
Map 14

Behind the slightly grim countenance of mills and factories, Silsden proves to be a surprisingly pleasant little town (or should that be, large village) attractively watered by a tributary of the Aire which skips along the High Street like a happy child.

VILUCCI - Kirkgate. Tel: 01535 656599. Cafe bar/deli.
STEFANO'S - Kirkgate. Tel: 01535 658555. Italian.
BRIDGE INN - canalside bridge 191A. Delightful pub which actually pre-dates the canal, harking back as far as the 17th century. Bar meals and Skipton-brewed Copper Dragon. Tel: 01535 653144. Families catered for. Exceptionally good FISH & CHIP shop next door.

Useful little shopping centre with NatWest & Barclays banks. Several good old fashioned retailers like HILLS the baker and SMITHIES the butcher.

TRAINS - station (Steeton & Silsden) lies a mile south-west of canal but there are frequent buses. Tel: 08457 484950.

SKIPTON
Map 13

Is Skipton the perfect, medium-sized town? Quite possibly yes! Self-styled as the "Gateway to the Dales", old 'Sheep Town' holds sway over the Aire Gap as it has done since the 7th century. We like it so much that it is never a chore to revisit to check details for updates. Its broad, typically Yorkshire High Street - pulsating with market stalls on most days - sprouts quieter, more intimate ginnels and courtyards, topographically estranged from the main thoroughfares in aloof oases of timeless calm.

BLACK HORSE HOTEL - High Street. Old coaching inn used for meetings by the L&L's promoters. Back bar overlooks Springs Branch. Tel: 01756 792145.
WOOLLY SHEEP - Sheep St. Friendly Timothy Taylor pub offering lunch, evening meals and bed & breakfast. Tel: 01756 700966.
ROYAL SHEPHERD - Canal Street. Charming muzak-free town pub overlooking Springs Branch Arm offering lunches, a peaceful garden, stained-glass with a canal theme, and an interesting range of authentic ales. Tel: 01756 793178.
THE NARROW BOAT - Victoria St. Quiet new bar; lunches and a wide range of interesting beers. Tel: 01756 797922.
BIZZIE LIZZIES - canalside (bridge 178) fish restaurant. Tel: 01756 701131.
EASTWOODS - ditto (bridge 179A). Tel: 01756 795458.
BAY HORSE - canalside at Snaygill (bridge 182). Solid, traditional Tetley pub with family room, garden and steak restaurant.

Shopping is Skipton's strongpoint and it has attracted the likes of Rackhams, Laura Ashley and the Edinburgh Woollen Mill to open branches here. The market flourishes on most weekdays. Many alleyways slink furtively away from the main street and issue into interesting courtyards, most notably CRAVEN COURT which, from a narrow entry, opens out into an airy rectangle covered by a graceful canopy of cast iron and glass. Sooner or later, though, most folk end up at STANFORTH'S, the "celebrated pork pie establishment", handily located for canal users by bridge 2 on the Spring's Branch, where the pies come warm, Yorkshire fashion, and the jelly 'explodes' in your mouth (and all down your clothes if you're not careful). Most banks have branches in the town and there are TESCO and MORRISONS supermarkets within easy reach of the canal.

TRAINS - excellent service southwards to Leeds and Bradford with handy stops along the Aire Valley for towpath walkers. Skipton can also be used as a launch pad for the Settle & Carlisle if you've time at your disposal. Tel: 08457 484950.

continued overleaf:

continued from previous page:

BUSES - Pennine run to Gargrave, Barnoldswick, Colne and Burnley. Tel: 01756 749215. For other operators services telephone 0870 6082608.

 TOURIST INFORMATION - Coach Street. Tel: 01756-792809.

THE CRAVEN MUSEUM - Town Hall, High Street. Tel: 01756 706407. Local history and travelling exhibitions.

SKIPTON CASTLE - The town's crowning glory. Superb 11th century fortification, though much domesticised down the years. Open daily from 10am (noon Sundays). Tel: 01756 792442.

EMBSAY STEAM RAILWAY - located at Embsay two miles east of town centre (bus connections). Delightful small steam line which runs as far as Bolton Abbey. Tel: 01756 794727 for operating details.

PENNINE BOAT TRIPS - Coach Street. Public trips and charters by wideboat. An excellent taster for the L&L if you're not already afloat. Tel: 01756 790829.

SLAITHWAITE   *Map 34*

The authentic pronounciation is akin to 'Slough-it' (as in "come friendly bombs and fall on Slough"). This typically attractive Colne Valley community currently features in the television drama *Where The Heart Is.*

MOONRAKER - floating tearoom housed in narrowboat moored above Lock E24. Closed Mondays. Tel: 01484 846370.

CAPTAIN'S TABLE - Carr Lane. Fish & chip restaurant (takeaways too) overlooking canal. Tel: 01484 841068.

MONSOON - canalside Britannia Road. Tandoori restaurant and takeaway open evenings daily. Tel: 01484 845818.

THE FULL MUFFIN - canalside Bridge Street. Tel: 01484 844646. Eat in or take out pies and sandwiches.

Lots of pubs plus even more takeaways and fish & chip shops as well.

Slaithwaite's array of waterside shops are difficult to resist, and they ooze with character too, from BLACKBURN'S long established gentleman's outfitters (where you can obtain that flat cap you'd always secretly promised yourself) to E. GRANGE & SON the butcher who makes his own award-winning pies and WALSH'S "High Class" greengrocer; the last two both being on Britannia Road. The CO-OP is open 8am to 10pm daily and there's a LLOYDS TSB bank with autoteller. Handy launderette as well. Researching this new edition, MERRYDALE FRESH FARM FOODS shop on Carr Lane also caught our eye.

COLNE VALLEY TRUST - information centre and gift shop. Tel: 01484 847790.

TRAINS - local services to/from Huddersfield, Stalybridge, Manchester etc. Tel: 08457484950.

BUSES - frequent connections through Colne Valley. Tel: 0113 245 7676.

SOWERBY BRIDGE   *Map 28*

For some reason, hard to fathom, Sowerby Bridge reminded us of Domodossola in the Italian Alps. Perhaps it was the boulder-strewn riverbed; or an empathetic similarity in the high buildings of indigenous stone, stacked precariously upon each other as if on the shelves of an untidy warehouse; or that same, slightly lugubrious sense of a workaday town hewn from a mountain fastness. But when we tried our hesitant Italian on the check-out girl at Kwik Save we got no response; though do you ever?

JAVA RESTAURANT - Wharf Street (opposite canal basin). Indonesia comes to the West Riding. Evenings only. Tel: 01422 831654.

THE MOORINGS - warehouse conversion at the canal basin. Tel: 01422 833940.

GIMBALS - Wharf Street. Tel: 01422 839329. Expensive but commensurately tempting restaurant.

KWIKSAVE handy by new deep lock. Lloyds, Barclays and Yorkshire banks. Market on Tue, Fri & Sat across the river beyond the railway bridge.

TRAINS - Calder Valley services from station easily reached by footpath and alleyway adjacent to fish & chip shop in Wharf Street. Tel: 08457 484950.

BUSES - Tel: 0113 245 7676.

STALYBRIDGE

Map 37

Another town made poorer by the passing of its trolleybuses, but 2001 will go down in the town's annals as the year Stalybridge's football team (The Celtic) were promoted and the town got its canal back. The footballers' success may prove ephemeral (it did!), but the impact on Stalybridge of the regenerated Huddersfield Canal will be considerable and lasting.

THE WELLINGTON (Tel: 0161 877 7440) and the WHARF TAVERN (Tel: 0161 338 2662) are handy locals by the tail of Lock 4W but to visit Stalybridge and not attend the STATION BUFFET (Tel: 0161 303 0007) would be tantamount to visiting Rome and not going to see the Vatican.

With SOMERFIELD and TESCO supermarkets adjacent to the canal you won't have far to go to replenish the stores, but don't just stick slavishly to their predictable lines, in Melbourne Street (which crosses the tail of Lock 6W) you'll find some characterful local shops with the emphasis on food like: FARM FOODS, SAY CHEESE (a really good deli), THE MEAT EMPORIUM and THE CHICKEN BARBECUE, the last of which reminded us of those outlets at Spanish seaside resorts where you can come away with a whole spit-grilled chicken ready to eat. A little lower down the street you'll find a cluster of banks - NatWest, Lloyds TSB, Yorkshire and Barclays.

TRAINS - good service to/from Manchester and Huddersfield and local Tame and Colne valley stations. Tel: 08457484950.
BUSES - Tel: 0161 228 7811.

TODMORDEN

Map 30

Nineteenth century Todmorden lay half in Lancashire, half in Yorkshire. The Town Hall - "classical, yet with a certain crisp and sensuous elegance" according to Pevsner - topped by sculpted figures representing the commerce of each county, straddled the boundary. It is typical of the town's rich roll call of fine Victorian buildings enhanced by its setting between the steep bifurcating valleys of the Calder and its tributary, Walsden Water. Working through Shop Lock, a woman popped her head round the corner and asked if we wanted our photograph taken as a group. They are that sort of friendly in 'Toddy', and she seemed genuinely disappointed when we told her we weren't exactly holidaymakers. But the really good thing about Todmorden - and a salutary lesson for tourist officers everywhere - is that it doesn't flaunt itself like Hebden Bridge tends to do. Of course this may just be sloth misinterpreted as modesty, but, to us at least, Todmorden came over as a warm, unmistakably 'northern' community. Local hero, John Fielden, is remembered by a statue in Centre Vale Park, recalling that he was largely responsible for the Ten Hours Act of 1847, a landmark in industrial reforms preventing employees from working more than a ten hour day which seems to have been conveniently forgotten.

THE BEAR - Rochdale Road (adjacent Library Lock). Vegetarian cafe located on first floor of former premises of Todmorden Industrial Co-operative store. Open daily. Wonderfully informal atmosphere complete with an unobtrusive children's play area and a comfortable sofa surrounded by vigorous potted plants where you can recover from the arduous Rochdale with generous lashings from the wholefood and vegetarian menu. Tel: 01706 819690.

ROSE & CROWN - on main road near Woodhouse Mill Bridge. Quaint stone pub offering good food, quiet and Taylor's Landlord. Tel: 01706 812428.

Yorkshire and Barclays banks. Wonderful indoor market, Safeway and Co-op supermarkets. Look out for TODMORDEN CRAFT CENTRE (adjacent Shop Lock) and THE BEAR'S (again!) ground floor wholefood shop.

TRAINS - half-hourly connections with Manchester (via Rochdale) and Leeds (via Halifax). Tel: 08457 484950. BUSES to/from Burnley.

TOURIST INFORMATION - Burnley Road. Tel: 01706 818181.

UPPERMILL

Map 36

The Tame chuckles picturesquely through this unexpectedly zestful former textile village which has transformed itself into something of a resort, all gift shops and tea rooms and coach parties wondering what to do. If they'd only look about them they'd find plenty. On Whit Friday the famous Saddleworth Brass Band Contest (as featured in *Brassed Off*) takes place whilst in August the Morris dancing Rush Cart Festival draws in the crowds.

JONATHAN'S - High Street. Tel: 01457 876976. Attractive bistro/cafe new since the last edition. Elsewhere there are tea rooms, tandooris, pubs and Italian restaurants galore.

Two secondhand-bookshops add interest to the rash of gift shops. More practically there's a NatWest bank with autoteller, a post office, chemist, and Co-op 'Late Shop'

SADDLEWORTH MUSEUM & ART GALLERY - fascinating little museum housed in the remains of a canalside mill; excellent and imaginative displays of local history. Tel: 01457 874093.

TOURIST INFORMATION - annex to above museum. Tel: 01457 870336.

WAKEFIELD
Map 23

Some places are greater than the sum of their parts. Wakefield is less. Though some of its parts are very pretty indeed. Garrotted by ring roads, and scarred by the acne-like rash of Sixties architecture, it suddenly hits you that this is Poulson territory, and so perhaps that is why Wakefield has a legacy of shoddy buildings. And yet, and yet, there are some absolutely wonderful buildings in Wakefield which are owed a better setting: the Cathedral (so well integrated now with the secular world of consumerland on its doorstep that it has won a major award); the Town Hall (so typical in its ebullient Victorian sense of permanence and provincial pride); and, of course, that marvellous Chantry Chapel (so redolent of the Middle Ages despite being compromised by the crass proximity of a modern concrete bridge) all deserve your admiration.

THE MILL HOUSE - canalside at Stanley Ferry (Map 22). Purpose-built 'complex' with real ales plus "Moorings Carvery" in conservatory decorated with archive canalia. Families well catered for. Tel: 01924 290596.

KINGS ARMS - Heath Common. Classic stone-floored, gas-lit country inn. Bar & restaurant meals. Clarks (of Wakefield) ales. Tel: 01924 377527.

The centre of Wakefield is ten minutes walk uphill from the river. The chainstores get their act together at THE RIDINGS. Alternatively you could try your luck at the huge retail market hall open daily (ex Suns).

TRAINS - stations at Westgate and Kirkgate: the former more important, with InterCity services to Leeds, London and the Midlands; the latter more handily placed for the river, and offering useful links for towpath walkers with Castleford, Mirfield and Huddersfield. Tel: 08457484950.

TOURIST INFORMATION - Town Hall. Tel: 01924 295000.

CITY TRAIL - a series of linked interpretive boards delving into the city's history. Starts on Wood Street. Excellent guide book available.

CATHEDRAL - holds claim to the highest spire in Yorkshire. Earliest parts date from 15th century.

ART GALLERY - Wentworth Terrace. Open daily. Noted for its collection of contemporary works.

WALSDEN
Map 30

Walsden snuggles cosily in its steep sided valley out of the worst that the moorland winds would otherwise throw at it. It's a mid Pennine community in microcosm, with textile mills and dyeworks (and a strange occupation called 'picker' making) taking advantage of the fast-flowing water supply, and with the scars of former quarrying on the slopes. They even dug coal from primitive shafts up on the tops, where the miners rubbed shoulders with hill farmers. The nomenclature resonates with the harshness of life: Top o' th' Rough, Rake End, Jail Hole, Foul Clough Road, Thorns Greece and Pot Oven. It's like another language. And perhaps it was, after all, 'Walsden' is said to derive from "Valley of the Welshmen."

VILLAGE CHIPPY - adjacent Hollings Lock. Queues down the street testify to the deliciousness of the Pollard family's fish & chips, and when at last you reach the counter, it is to have your inner man satisfied by a bevy of lovely ladies.

HOLLINS INN - uphill from Hollings Lock. Modernised stone-built pub dating back to 1708. Food, families and Theakstons. Tel: 01706 817105.

Newsagents adjacent to Hollings Lock. Post office adjacent Travis Mill Lock.

TRAINS - hourly, daily services linking Walsden with useful towpath-walking stages at Littleborough and Rochdale to the south and Todmorden and Hebden Bridge to the north. Tel: 08457 484950.

WHEELTON
Map 3

Quaint village of redbrick terraces with a piquant clock-towered war memorial. Sadly the general store and fish & chip shop are recent examples of the remorselessly ebbing tide of village economic decline, but the post office clings on (selling crafts as a side line) and there's an off licence and launderette for alcoholic boaters with lock grease stains on their clothes. The TOP LOCK by Bridge 58 is a Camra recommended pub offering "good homemade food". Tel: 01257 263376. Timothy Taylor on tap.

WIGAN
Map 1

Terracotta and concrete collide as, with one foot firmly in the past, Wigan attempts to shed its unwanted and unwarrented Orwellian legacy, yet maximise returns from the profitable nostalgia business.Sometimes you sense the past suffocates the present like parents unwilling to let a child step out of their shadow. But the sheer warmth and good humour of Wigan folk (and their lovely dialect) transcends such a reactionary outlook, and you go back to your boat happy in the knowledge that you have rubbed shoulders with a 'real' town.

THE ORWELL - canalside at Wigan Pier. Warehouse conversion offering lunches and a decent range of real ale. Tel: 01942 323034.

KIRKLESS HALL - canalside Lock 66. Tel: 01942 242821. Much revitalised canalside inn offering a wide range of food and some eminently quaffable real ales such as Wadworth 6X. These laudable improvements have brought a fresh sense of security to the area.

THE COMMERCIAL INN - canalside bridge 57 near top of Wigan 21. Was under new management as we went to press. Tel: 01942 238856.

CRAWFORD ARMS - canalside bridge 63 at Red Rock. Comfortable country pub. Food, families welcome. Tel: 01257 421313.

The town centre is 5-10 minutes walk from Wigan Pier. Chain stores at THE GALLERIES, more individual retailers at the MARKET HALL. Stock the galley up, bearing in mind that you may be spending a fullish day leaving Wigan.

TRAINS - North Western station for InterCity; Wallgate for most local traffic. Tel: 08457 484950. BUSES - useful half-hourly, Mon-Sat service (362) connects with Chorley (not directly linked with Wigan by rail). Tel: 0870 6082608.

TOURIST INFORMATION - Trencherfield Mill, Wigan Pier. Tel: 01942 825677.

WIGAN PIER - open daily ex Fri. Tel: 01942 323666. Highly popular visitor centre recreating Wigan's 19th century industrial and domestic heyday. A frequent waterbus links the main exhibition centre with Trencherfield Mill which features Opie's Museum of Memories and the world's largest textile mill engine.

HISTORY SHOP - Library Street. Heritage centre with well stocked shop. Tel: 01942 827594.

WOODEND
Map 36

Little Tame Valley community between Greenfield and Mossley with no less than two Italian restaurants (LA QUILLA - Tel: 01457 839666 and TRATTORIA ROMA - Tel: 01457 833495) and two pubs (ROACHES LOCK - Tel: 01457 834288 and TOLLEMARCH ARMS - Tel: 01457 832354) a fish & chip shop and a general store.

WOODLESFORD
Map 20

Very useful staging post between Leeds and Castleford. Two pubs and a Chinese takeaway in the centre of the village, seven or eight minutes walk (uphill) from the visitor moorings at Swillington Bridge. Post office stores and newsagent. Good local train services - Tel: 08457 484950.

How to use the Maps

There are thirty-seven numbered maps. Maps 1 to 19 cover the Leeds & Liverpool Canal between Wigan (where it links with Pearson's Cheshire Ring Canal Companion) and Leeds; maps 19 to 23 cover the Aire & Calder Navigation between Leeds and Wakefield via Castleford; maps 23 to 28 cover the Calder & Hebble Navigation between Wakefield and Sowerby Bridge; maps 28 to 31 cover the Rochdale Canal between Sowerby Bridge and Littleborough; and maps 32 to 37 cover the Huddersfield Broad and Narrow canals between Cooper Bridge and Ashton-under-Lyne.

All the maps can be used equally well in either direction. The simplest way of progressing from map to map is to proceed to the next map numbered from the edge of the map you are on. Figures quoted at the top of each map refer to distance per map, locks per map and average cruising times. An alternative indication of timings from centre to centre can be found on the Route Planner inside the front cover. Obviously, cruising times vary with the nature of your boat and the number of crew at your disposal, so quoted times should be taken only as an estimate. Neither do times quoted take into account any delays which might occur at lock flights in the high season.

Using the Text

Each map is accompanied by a route commentary. Details of most settlements passed through are given alphabetically in the Gazetteer. Regular readers will already be familiar with our somewhat irreverant approach. But we 'tell it how we find it', in the belief that users find this attitude more valuable than a strict towing of the tourist publicity line. Boating facilities are grouped on page 93.

Towpath Walking

The most fundamentally simple way of getting to know the canals covered by this guide is on foot. This is how our research begins. One foot in front of another. And for once, our towpath condition categories were almost superfluous, for we found the towpaths of the Leeds & Liverpool, Aire & Calder, Calder & Hebble, Rochdale and Huddersfield canals uniformly good. In fact, the only problems

we encountered were following heavy winter bouts of rain when the quality of the surface was almost too good in places for the excess water to drain away; and the absence of towpath on one or two stretches of the Aire & Calder and Calder & Hebble. In the latter instance, we have tried to indicate on the maps the most convenient or appropriate detour.

Happily, public transport parallels the waterways covered in most places. Legs of ten or twelve miles are easily organised. Our lengthiest research walk was between Colne and Skipton, though this could easily have been broken up by using the bus to Barnoldswick. When using public transport to facilitate a one-way towpath walk, we always advise two things: 1 Check the timetable by telephone. 2 Always assuming you're reasonably fit and are sure of completing the distance required, use the train or bus on the outward leg so that you are not necessarily pressured to complete the walk by a certain time.

Towpath Cycling

Cycling access to towpaths is an activity in its infancy, and British Waterways are only just beginning to come to terms with the concept of cycling for pleasure. To ride the towpaths you must first obtain a permit from one of the British Waterways offices listed on page 90. With the permit (which is free of charge) will come a list of approved sections for cycling on. No permit is required for cycling on the towpath of the privately-owned Rochdale Canal.

Boating

Boating on the waterways covered by this guide has never really taken off in the way that it has on the traditional canals of the Midlands. Received wisdom suggests that these waterways are perceived as 'difficult' by the boating classes. "Too hard for a holiday!" We beg to differ. Well, there's an element of truth in that - as you will see from the text - but show us a canal route (with the possible exception of the Llangollen, Oxford and Shropshire Union) which doesn't encounter an industrial landscape somewhere or other in its travels: why else would they have been built? So let Pearsons debunk the myth and gently encourage you to make an exploration by boat of these wonderfully diverse, and richly charactered "Pennine Waters".

Navigational Advice
LEEDS & LIVERPOOL CANAL
The chief characteristics of this canal are its wide-beam locks (62ft x 14ft) and its swingbridges. Both have a largely unwarranted reputation for being hard graft, and we encountered no particular problems other than the frustration of having to unlock and relock the vandal-proof 'handcuff' locks attached to a good number of the lock paddles and the majority of the swingbridges. These are fitted to prevent vandalism, though you do begin to wonder, in some of the more remote and rural locations in which they are fitted, what self-respecting hooligan is likely to wander so far from the nearest glue counter. The Leeds & Liverpool's broad locks are able to assimilate two narrowboats side by side, and as most of the craft using this canal these days seem to fall into this category, it makes sense to share locks where feasible, both for the sake of saving water and also from the aspect of saving energy. Turbulence can be a problem in wide locks when travelling uphill. Some boaters prefer to use ropes (looped around the mid-lock bollard) to steady their craft. Insouciant to a fault, we tend to simply draw the paddle on the same side as the boat first, which has the effect of bouncing off the opposite lock wall and holding the boat more or less against the side it's on. Whatever your preferred method, use the ground paddles first until the lock is at least half full. Mention of ground paddles brings to mind the weird and wonderful variety of gear still extant on the Leeds & Liverpool. Don't be nervous of them, survivals like cloughs (clows), box paddles and gate 'scissors' are to be cherised in this age of uniformity and you will soon get the hang of them.

Individually the lock flights of the L&L have their own characteristics. British Waterways no longer offer formally to accompany boaters through Wigan Locks - as was once the case - but lock staff are usually on hand during working hours should you require assistance. There are no particular problems associated with the picturesque locks at Johnson's Hillock. Blackburn Locks usually have a lock-keeper in attendance. His office is at Nova Scotia Wharf. Barrowford Locks were running heavy when we encountered them in March, but this may have just been a phenonomen associated with a wet Spring. The rural flights at Greenberfield, Bank Newton and Gargrave gave us no trouble at all. The risers at Bingley are looked after by an enthusiastic keeper who's always prepared to impart a good deal of knowledgeable and worthwhile advice while he oversees your passage through. The various groups of locks between Bingley and Leeds tend to be quite arduous, and it's important to hone your 'staircase' technique by making sure that the chamber below you is sufficiently empty (about a 'quarter full' was recommended to us) to receive the water from the chamber you are in. Likewise, going uphill, the chamber above you should be full so as to allow it to be emptied to fill the chamber you are in.

Swingbridges on the Leeds & Liverpool fall into three distinct categories. Most are manually operated by brute strength, a few (Maps 6 & 16) require the use of a windlass, whilst a handful in the vicinity of Keighley, and one at Skipton and Apperley Bridge, are electrified and controlled from a push-button console accessed with the BW sanitary station Yale key. You'll have read (Map 15) about our problems with the latter, but then machinery always was a mystery to us, and nine times out of ten you'll have no trouble with them. The secret is to ensure that each stage of the sequence is completed and that the bridge has fully returned to its closed position before attempting to extract the key.

AIRE & CALDER NAVIGATION
Being, until recently at least, a fully-fledged commercial waterway, the Aire & Calder is perceived as a 'whole new ball game' by most boaters. That's true, of course, but, if gone about correctly and with due care and respect - particularly if commercial craft are encountered - it can also be enormous fun, an exhilarating change from other, more modestly engineered canals. Bear in mind, too, that this is a 'navigation' with sections of river where the current can conjure up tricks that no canal - however magical aesthetically - can match. Hazard areas for current are: below Leeds River Lock where the full force of the Aire sluicing through the Dark Arches can make life difficult when entering or leaving the lock; and at Leeds Dam where there can be a considerable draw away from the navigational channel. The newest hazard to cruising the Aire & Calder is the provision of push-button controls for boater operation of the locks. Again operated by BW's Yale key, there is (theoretically) a simple six step sequence
continued overleaf:

continued from previous page:

(maximum) for operating these locks in the absence of a lock-keeper. Should there be a malfunction, a lock-side telephone can be used to call for help.

CALDER & HEBBLE NAVIGATION

C&H locks (57ft 6ins x 14ft) tend to fill very quickly in our experience. Ensure you use the ground paddles first, though at some locks you may find only a gate paddle, in which case it should be opened only a little at a time so as to minimise turbulence. A characteristic of the Calder & Hebble is the provision of flood locks at the upstream end of the navigation cuts, constructed to bypass various meanders of the river. Unless the river is in flood, these 'locks' will be open to passing boats. After heavy rain, however, they may need to be closed. At such times boats should remain in the safety of the cuts, not passing down on to the river until the colour marker gauge at the tail of the lock is at least yellow, and preferably green.

On Map 24 we draw your attention to 'handspikes', not some diabolical instrument of torture left over from the Spanish Inquisition, but rather, a piece of timber (not unlike a baseball bat) which you insert into a cog and make a series of manual wrench-like movements to raise the paddle. After your initial nervousness has worn off you begin to look forward to showing your prowess at this technique, though we were never able to fathom a method of lowering the paddle gently, so we simply extracted the handspike and let the paddle fall.

ROCHDALE CANAL

Now under British Waterways control, the Rochdale can prove challenging, but rewarding. New 'plastic' paddle gear is progressively being fitted to its locks, and the provision of by-weirs at the locks will help to equate water levels in the intervening pounds. The deep lock at Tuel Lane, Sowerby Bridge, is likely to be manned at most times of the day.

HUDDERSFIELD NARROW CANAL

Freshly restored, there are teething troubles associated with the Huddersfield Narrow Canal which demand a degree of patience from the boater. Don't expect to travel at your usual average pace along this lock heavy canal. This is 'wild west' boating and you may need to make up the script as you go along. Maximum lock dimensions are 70ft x 6ft 10ins and we have heard that traditional craft are unlikely to pass through easily if at all. All the locks west of Standedge, and some to the east, are anti-vandal locked. Passage of Standedge Tunnel (a tug hauls your boat) must be pre-booked on 01977 554351.

Moorings

An 'open' bollard symbol represents visitor mooring sites; either as designated specifically by British Waterways or, in some cases, as recommended by our own personal experience. Of course, one of the great joys of canal boating has always been the ability to moor almost wherever (sensibly) you like; though, in recent years, it has become obvious that, particularly in urban areas, there are an increasing number of undesirable locations where mooring is not to be recommended for fear of vandalism, theft or abuse. We hope, therefore, that you find our suggestions both pleasant and secure. But do bear in mind that the absence of a bollard symbol from any particular location does not necessarily imply that it is unsuitable or not to be recommended.

Useful Contacts

British Waterways were re-organised into ten new territories at the end of 2003. The canals in this guide are split into the North West and Yorkshire regions. British Waterways North West Region office is located at Trafalgar House, Temple Court, Birchwood, Warrington WA3 6GD Tel: 01925 847700. It covers the Leeds & Liverpool west of Bridge 158 at Greenberfield (Map 10), the Rochdale Canal, and the Huddersfield Canal west of Standedge.

All the other waterways covered in Pennine Waters come under the jurisdiction of British Waterways Yorkshire Waterways at Fearns Wharf, Neptune Street, Leeds LS9 8PB. Tel: 0113 281 6800.

Closures

Closures - known as 'stoppages' on the canals - usually occur between November and April when maintenance work is undertaken. Occasionally, however, an emergency stoppage may be imposed at short notice. Up to date details are usually available from hire bases. British Waterways provide a recorded message service for private boaters. The number to ring is: 01923-201401. Stoppages are also listed on British Waterways' web site at *www.britishwaterways.co.uk*

Todmorden, Rochdale Canal

Emergencies

Outside office hours, British Waterways operate a central emergency telephone service. Dial the operator and ask for FREEPHONE CANALS. For mobile phone users the number is 0800 47 999 47.

Societies

The Inland Waterways Association was founded in 1946 to campaign for retention of the canal system. Many routes now open to pleasure boaters might not have been available but for this organisation. Membership details may be obtained from: Inland Waterways Association, PO Box 114 Rickmansworth WD3 1ZY. Tel: 01923 711114.

Acknowledgements

Huge thanks to Brian Collings for yet another inspired cover; to Toby Bryant of Central Waterways Supplies; to Karen Tanguy, and to all at STIGE.

Mapping reproduced by permission of Ordnance Survey on behalf of The Controller of Her Majesty's Stationery Office, Crown Copyright 100033032

Lock 30E, Huddersfield Canal

Boat Yards

APPERLEY BRIDGE MARINA - Leeds & Liverpool Canal Map 17. Tel: 01274 616961.

ASPLEY WHARF MARINA - Huddersfield Broad Canal. Map 32. Tel: 01484 514123.

BALTIMORE MARINA - Rochdale Canal. Map 30. Tel: 01706 818973.

CLASSIC NARROWBOATS - Leeds & Liverpool Canal. Map 3. Tel: 01772 30640.

FALLWOOD MARINA - Leeds & Liverpool Canal Map 18. Tel: 0113 258 1074.

HAINSWORTH'S BOATYARD - Leeds & Liverpool Canal. Map 16. Tel: 01274 565925.

HAPTON BOATYARD - Leeds & Liverpool Canal. Map 7. Tel: 01282 773178

PICKWELL & ARNOLD - Rochdale Canal. Map 30. Tel: 01706 812411.

ROBINSONS - Calder & Hebble Navigation. Map 25. Tel: 01924 467976.

RODLEY BOAT CENTRE - Leeds & Liverpool Canal. Map 18. Tel: 0113 257 6132.

SAGAR MARINE - Calder & Hebble Navigation. Map 26. Tel: 01484 714541.

STANLEY FERRY MARINA - Aire & Calder Navigation. Map 22. Tel: 01924 201117.

SWIFTCRAFT - Leeds & Liverpool Canal. Map 17. Tel: 01274 611786.

WAKEFIELD BOAT CENTRE - Calder & Hebble Navigation. Map 23. Tel: 01924 366616.

WHITE BEAR MARINA - Leeds & Liverpool Canal. Map 2. Tel: 01257 481054

Hire Bases

ANGLO-WELSH - Leeds & Liverpool Canal Map 14. Tel: 0117 304 1122. www.anglowelsh.co.uk

LOWER PARK MARINA - Leeds & Liverpool Canal Map 10. Tel: 01282 815883.

PENNINE CRUISERS - Leeds & Liverpool Canal Map 13. Tel: 01756 795478. www.penninecruisers.com

SHEPLEY BRIDGE MARINA - Calder & Hebble Navigation Map 25. Tel: 01924 491872.

SHIRE CRUISERS - Calder & Hebble Navigation / Rochdale Canal Map 28. Tel: 01422 832712. www.shirecruisers.co.uk

SILSDEN BOATS - Leeds & Liverpool Canal Map 14. Tel: 01535 653675. www.silsdenboats.co.uk

SNAYGILL BOATS - Leeds & Liverpool Canal Map 13. Tel: 01756 795150. www.snaygillboats.co.uk

Standedge Tunnel, western portal

Plan Your Next Holiday Now!

We all know that sinking feeling as the boatyard approaches - the end of another great cruise. Now's the time to start thinking about the next trip, and what better way to plan ahead than with a Canal Companion. Nip into the shop or chandlery and get one before you leave for home. It'll do wonders for your sinking morale. There are eight more in the series; so collectible with their fabulous Brian Collings' 'sign-written' covers. Trust us with your next journey - afoot or afloat. We'll inform, entertain, and encourage your appreciation of the passing scene to the full. Here's to the next time!

PS - If you've any friends not yet bitten by the canal bug, why not take home a copy of *The Wonder of the Waterways*, a colourful introduction to the magic world of the canals compiled by Michael Pearson and featuring some of the best 'out-takes' from his photographic library, pictures which lack of space prevented from appearing in the Canal Companions themselves. A4 in format, and a 'steal' at just £4.99, buy one (or two, or three ...) now!

Available from hire bases, chandleries and canal gift shops, selected bookshops, Hoseasons, IWA, Amazon, Ian Allan etc or, in case of difficulty, direct from the publishers, Central Waterways Supplies, 32 Webb Ellis Industrial Park, Woodside Park, Rugby CV21 2NP. Telephone 01788 546692 or email sales@centralwaterways.co.uk to place your order.

Waterways World

the *NUMBER ONE* inland waterways magazine

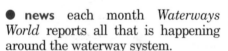

● **news** each month *Waterways World* reports all that is happening around the waterway system.

● **canal heritage** restoration reports, waterway history - the boats, people and companies that worked and built the canal system.

● **boat sales** more boats for sale every month than any other inland waterway magazine.

● **practical advice** for boat owners and aspiring boat owners - new and used narrowboat reviews, engine development, the latest equipment narrowboat fit-outs and much more.

● **enjoyment of the waterways** explore a different waterway each month with cruising reports, events, hire boat reviews, continental cruising.

Available from newsagents, boatyards and on subscription

Published by Waterways World Ltd, 151 Station Street, Burton-on-Trent, Staffs DE14 1BG   Telephone 01283 742970